We Are Not Seeing It

How & Why Mainstream Schools Break SEND Kids

By Luisa Gray
(aka. @LongRoadSENDMum)

WE ARE NOT SEEING IT

Cover design by toullacreative.com

First published in Great Britain in 2024

ISBN (Paperback): 9798341428003
Imprint: Independently published

Acknowledgements

This book would not exist without Little Sis & Big Bruv. Thank you for lighting up the world and teaching me all about who you are. Still learning every day! Love you love you.

To LongRoadDad: thank you for putting up with my hyperfocus days, for being my most supportive and most favourite reader, and for all the tea and roast dinners.

To GF: thank you for showing us that doors can be kicked open, and how to do it.

To AD: thank you for believing ever since junior school!

Big shout out to Fierce Mamma L, and Claude Queen E (two of the most tenacious people, who you absolutely want on your team!) and to The Core (F, K, S & S - you know who you are). Thank you all for just getting it, for never giving in even when things get too much, for being round the kitchen table and for sharing some bloody great coffee.

And finally a huge thank you to everyone who has ever interacted with my @LongRoadSENDMum Blog. Your well of kindness, support and love have saved my heart and mind on more occasions than you will ever know.

I couldn't have got this far, or written this book, without all of you being there to listen, share stories, inspire me, laugh and cry with.

Thank you x

WE ARE NOT SEEING IT

Contents

PART TWO

© The Long Road

Before we begin ...

Just so we're all absolutely clear, you'll see this punch line in a lot of my sketches.

I do not recommend or condone anyone telling anyone to piss off. It's just a cartoon punch line.

Thanks.

WE ARE NOT SEEING IT

Preface

I'm going to talk a lot about mainstream education, teachers, TA's, schools and sometimes even Local Authorities in this book.

And many teachers, education professionals and Local Authorities are not going to like what I have to say – because what I intend this book to do is explain how and why teachers, education professionals and Local Authorities are **hiding in plain sight, as probably the biggest drivers of the crisis SEND families all over the UK are currently in.**

If you work in a Local Authority commissioning team, or you are an education professional in a mainstream school and you want to genuinely understand, not just my family's experiences of the UK education system but also those of the thousands of parents who have engaged with my @LongRoadSENDMum blog over the years, read on: you're welcome, and I hope this will help you understand our families' struggles a little better.

If that isn't what you want, close this book now. I'm not asking anyone's permission (and I make no apologies whatsoever) for writing about what my family's truth is; it is the truth of many thousands of other SEND families too.

Terry Deary, the author of the Horrible Histories series once wrote:

"I don't believe in schools! I think all teachers should be sacked!"

And for a large proportion of them, I'm pretty much with him.

I know that's a pretty brutal assessment. And I know, as I wrote the majority of this book before the 2024 General Election and at a time when neither retention of existing teachers, or recruitment of enough new ones (either good or bad!) seemed even remotely possible, that my comments may not be welcome. But I stand by that brutal assessment, because it is not one I've simply plucked out of the air: it has come from real, lived experience.

So I don't have to keep labouring this point throughout the book, let me set out very clearly in this Preface:

- I don't believe for one second that any teacher or education professional goes into their profession **actively intending** to cause actual harm to a child's self-esteem or emotional and mental wellbeing

- I don't believe Local Authority employees go into their jobs **actively intending** to break SEND laws which are really clear, and actually really robust, thus compounding the damage being done to SEND children

- **But a huge number are doing exactly that**

Because …

- They do not understand what Special Educational Needs & Disabilities really look like

- They do not understand what their own professional obligations are under the Law

- **They do not understand the devastating impact their failures have on SEND families**

blah
…

Talking,
not listening

©The Long Road

I draw teachers, SENCOs and school heads in my blog like this:

This Teacher character represents all those terrible teachers and TAs, early years practitioners, SENCOs, heads, governors, and the general school culture that our family has met on our journey:

- institutionalised / old fashioned / stuck in their ways
- mouth open

- eyes shut
- talking, but definitely <u>not</u> listening!

Teachers, you may well argue that perhaps I've just come across a few "rogue ones" in my time. Yep, maybe I have. But here's the point:

- If the same patterns, and the same techniques, and the same phrases and the same problems keep coming up time and time again - **even when SEND children have changed schools to try to escape those systemic problem** - that is <u>not</u> an occasional "rogue" teacher

- **That is a professional <u>culture</u>**

- It's a culture that has been reinforced by
  - blinkered approaches to teacher training
  - bad policy from successive Governments
  - schools not upholding the law
  - and by LA Officers not upholding the law either / turning a blind eye to bad practice in their local mainstream schools

It's a culture that's causing untold damage to thousands of SEND children, every single day.

Too many education and LA professionals have either become:

- too absorbed in professional "Group Think"
- too arrogant and assured in their own "rightness"
- too bound to Government policy on education

Or they are closing their eyes to SEND in their classroom, through their own ignorance of

  - what Special Educational Needs & Disabilities are
  - what they really look like
  - how they really present
  - what they mean for a child/family
  - **and what their own lawful obligations actually are**

The same applies to Council / Local Authority (LA) officers working in SEND and Children's Directorates all over the country. The lack of basic knowledge of SEND law that I have experienced in LA officers is truly staggering. These are the people charged with commissioning EHC Needs Assessments (EHCNA – more on those later), writing our kids' lawfully-binding Education Health & Care Plans (EHCPs – more on those later too) and commissioning services for SEND kids, yet who largely do not know even the basics of the Statutory timeframes they should adhere to - and even when they do know, they seem remarkably relaxed about stretching those timeframes way beyond the Statutory limits. The attitude is very often "Well, what are you going to do about it? <u>Make</u> us stick to the lawful timelines! If you can .."

Nor do these LA officers seem to have the slightest grasp on the vital, lawfully-enforceable, and deeply personal nature of the work they are doing.

- I have seen EHCPs with needs described in Section B, and provision written in F (Section F is the lawfully binding bit) that look more like a "nice to have" wish list, than a Statutory document explicitly describing what the child's needs actually are, and the provision required to meet them.
- I've seen EHCPs containing spelling mistakes and basic typing errors - completely unacceptable in a legal document
- I've seen EHCP working documents where the LA has changed text between Draft versions, and <u>not highlighted</u> the changes they have made (either through simple human error/lack of attention, or perhaps more worryingly because they are hoping parents will not notice?)
- I have even seen EHCPs that have so obviously been produced by "cut & paste" that they get the child's sex wrong, and sometimes have even featured *a completely different child's name*

The blank look, or the shrug of the shoulders, that so often comes when you mention these unforgivable and unnecessary errors to an LA officer says more about their attitude to your child's very real needs than a bomb going off in your face.

And as for the fight to request additional funding ..? Don't even get me started.

What is just as striking as the attitude of commissioning officers, is the genuine lack of curiosity - both from council executives and elected councillors, as to:

- what LA commissioning officers and/or mainstream schools are doing when it comes to SEND
- why commissioning teams seem to suddenly be "over-spending" at such an alarming rate
- what might be driving that surge in what everyone in LAs loves to refer to as "demand" (as opposed to what it really is – i.e. "need")
- and what their own lawful obligations as elected councillors or executives might actually be

I draw LA officers in my blog like this.

I characterise them this way because LA officers hold the keys to The System: the funding and services SEND children need and are lawfully entitled to. Trying to access those services feels nothing like an entitlement at all, and far more like to laying solo siege to a fortress - a fortress that is far bigger than you, more powerful than you, that is designed to look impregnable enough to scare you off, and that will do anything it can to resist you getting to its treasures: i.e. the funding and services your child is *lawfully entitled* to, in order for them to thrive in any mainstream school.

The facts, though, remain the facts:

- **If you work for a Council, or in the Education sector, <u>you</u> are a Public Servant**
  - That means you are obliged to uphold **The Nolan Principles of Public Life:** Selflessness, Integrity, Objectivity, Accountability, Honesty, Openness and Leadership

(Source: https://www.gov.uk/government/publications/the-7-principles-of-public-life/the-7-principles-of-public-life--2)

But also – and VERY importantly:

- **Whoever is creating the problem, or how, or why, the harm caused to SEND children is the same. And it is massive, with potentially life-long repercussions.**

If you are a teacher, a SENCO, an LA officer, or anyone else involved in SEND as your job, and you have read those sentences and don't want to engage with me on my terms, that's fine.

Close the book and walk away.

But before you do, please ask yourself one question: If you're in these professions and you don't want to hear this message from a parent who has witnessed and fought the impact of my children's SEND needs being ignored for the best part of 11 years and counting...

Maybe <u>you're</u> part of the problem?

Anyway, once more for absolute clarity:

- **I <u>know</u> it is not ALL teachers and not all TAs** who are failing to recognise or support children with SEND needs. (I can name every single one of the wonderful teachers and TAs who have actually supported and tried to help my kids, and I will love each one of them forever)

- I **know** it is not ALL SENCOs, not all Heads, not all schools who are "not seeing it", thereby exacerbating problems and creating trauma for children with SEND

- I **know** it is not all LA officers who are wilfully ignoring need, or knowingly behaving unlawfully

• But far too many are

I get it: Teachers, TAs, Heads, SENCOS are all human beings. Many are horribly overworked and under-valued by an education system that does not adequately train or support them.

Again, I get it. Local Authority commissioning officers are human beings, who are struggling under an avalanche of newly-recognised Special Educational Needs and Disabilities, often without the proper training, knowledge of the law, or funding available to meet all these needs.

Having said that, both LongRoadDad and I would argue very strongly that **any job or profession is ultimately a choice**.

- Education staff *can* choose to upskill and learn

- Local Authority officers *can* do the same

- Service Directors and councillors *can* tell the truth. Whistleblow if needs be.

  o They have the power to stop their Council fighting parents through the Tribunals system, and instead shine a light on the desperate state of the SEND services in their area

  o They and their bosses have the power to make central Government take this problem seriously, and provide the funding that's required to meet the rising levels of need (instead of framing SEND families' lawful and very real needs as "increased demand").

- Should they wish to or need to, all these professionals _can_ choose to change to a different career. Many do, when the pressure they feel they are under gets too much.

But a SEND child cannot choose to stop being a SEND child, or to stop having the significant needs they have.

And a SEND parent cannot choose to stop being a SEND parent, or to un-see our child's needs once we have begun to really understand them.

Whether a teacher, or a TA, or SENCO, or a Head, or a Local Authority employee likes it or not, it really is their professional obligation to step up and do their lawful duty for the SEND children in their care.

Sadly though, far too many do the opposite.

OK, I've said my piece.
Let's move on.

"ONE DOESN'T HAVE TO
OPERATE WITH GREAT
MALICE TO DO GREAT
HARM.
THE ABSENCE OF EMPATHY
& UNDERSTANDING ARE
SUFFICIENT."

———

CHARLES M. BLOW

PART ONE

My Kids Are Being Bullied. And So Am I.

If your kids have any type of Special Educational Needs or Disability - especially an invisible one like autism, or dyspraxia/DCD, or dyslexia, or sensory processing disorder, or ADHD, or mental health difficulties - then I'll bet your kids, and you as their parents, are being bullied too.

I'm not talking about the playground bully who calls you names and nicks your dinner money. I'm talking about something that's far more sinister, and a lot harder to spot.

I'm talking about the UK mainstream school system bullying families, to make it pretty much impossible for SEND kids like mine (and yours) to remain in mainstream school.

For some families, that's not always a bad thing. Many SEND kids really *can't* thrive in mainstream school from day 1: their needs are too complex for that setting, and those children really will learn and thrive best in a specialist setting. But places in those settings are *incredibly* difficult for SEND families to access: years upon years of service and funding cuts under the guise of "austerity" or "streamlining" or whatever buzzword those in charge wanted to use, mean there simply are not enough services or specialist school places or money to go round. So in spite of overwhelming need, a lot of SEND kids are trapped in mainstream schools, with their needs going unrecognised and unmet, year after year.

Some families want to Electively Home Educate (EHE) or use EOTAS (Education Other Than at School). Flexischooling is another option. For many SEND families (and non-SEND families too), that's the way they feel their child can learn best. I'm not going to go into these different options in any great depth in this book; they really need a book all to themselves, and there are lots of very good ones already out there. All I will say is if these are what families want to do, and it's an **active choice** on your part, then I'm genuinely happy for you, and I wish everyone on those paths the very best of success.

But an increasing number of families are finding:

- even if EHE or EOTAS is not the ideal option

- and even if something like EHE wouldn't necessarily meet the child's needs or their particular learning style

- or even if the parents themselves know in their hearts that they are just not cut out for home educating their child ...

- their child has been ground down to such a point of wreckage, that there's **no other choice left** but to take their SEND kids out of mainstream school

Where does that leave the SEND kids who want and really need the structure of being at school?
What about the kids who really get a buzz from the school environment, who love the social aspect of school, and who would potentially be left feeling shut out and isolated if they left?
They still deserve to have that option of being at a school.

What about the kids like mine who, on paper, and with the right support in place, really ought to have thrived in mainstream school ... but who really, really haven't been able to?

And what about parents like LongRoadDad and I?

- If I'd wanted to be (and had actually been suited to being!) a teacher, I would have trained as one years ago when I had the opportunity

- Between them, Big Bruv and Little Sis have a detailed list of Special Educational Needs.   Not just needs: Educational needs.

- Most importantly of all, our kids do not want us to be their teacher!
  - School is school, home is home
  - **Our kids want us to be their mum and dad** - not their educators!

As a family, we do have a right to make those choices.

We do have a right to protect that exclusively parental relationship with our kids.

We also have a right <u>not</u> to be forced into a teacher/educator relationship with our children, just because the education system is <u>choosing</u> to fail them.

Yet SEND families are being given very few other choices by the mainstream school system. And that is where my family, and probably yours, are being systematically bullied.

Because some mainstream schools want SEND kids out of their settings. Completely.

Image Credit: SkyNews.com Source tps://news.sky.com/story/amp/pupils-exclusion-trauma-revealed-as-some-schools-remove-special-needs-students-to-protect-results-13008254

There is even a name for this practice. As Sky News revealed in a November 2023 "whistleblower" article, actively forcing SEND kids out of mainstream schools to protect exam results is called **"Intelligence Cleansing"**.

Not only is "Intelligence Cleansing" a disturbing trend that smacks of .. well let's just say other types of "cleansing" that have taken place against people in minorities throughout history: it is also a

massive problem for the thousands upon thousands of families ~ like mine ~ who are
trying to resist this almost irresistible push to leave a school, once the school has decided it doesn't want a SEND child (or their parents) causing them problems anymore.

If you've been there yourself, you know which tactics I'm talking about that make the push irresistible. If you haven't yet, here's a quick checklist:

- Your child's teacher repeatedly tells you everything is fine
- The SENCO tells you that everything is fine: everything to support your child/in your child's plan (if they have one) is being done. There is nothing to worry about, and your child is actually really, really happy in school
- The Deputy Head repeats that message
- So does the Head
- The school starts limiting your access (e.g. only offering short meetings, where you cannot address all your concerns because there is not enough time)
- You cannot get a meeting with anyone senior in the school - instead you're being offered "chats" with pastoral staff or TAs (people who may mean well, but who have no actual power to change anything for your child at all)
- If you do manage to get a meeting, random people are there without you having being told beforehand (basically to make sure there are "more of us" than there are of you. A school or academy so-called "Improvement Officer" - who you never even knew existed until they magically appear in a "friendly chat" meeting - is a particular favourite "random invitee")
- The SENCO eventually stops returning your calls / becomes "too busy" to speak with you at all
- The Head stops replying to your calls / emails
- The Governors decline to meet you, or tell you they have investigated your complaints and they have "absolute confidence" that everything is fine

- You get told you are "over-communicating", and are asked to stop emailing or calling (or the school tries to impose restrictions on your communication)
- You are told you are "upsetting" members of staff, which is affecting their mental health
- In extreme cases, I've heard of parents being told they can no longer come into the school, or even set foot on the school premises
- Parents are - either by implication / veiled threat, or directly and explicitly - told by a school to "off-roll" their child (i.e. de-register their child and Electively Home Educate them instead), because the school "cannot meet need".
- **This is unlawful, and both schools, and Local Authorities know it is unlawful.** But it still happens anyway.

Once a school has decided to turn on a family and close down, there is very little that family can do, unless they have the resources to bring in an Advocate / launch a legal fight - or move to EHE.

But EHE often still doesn't solve the problem of unmet need for many families (it wouldn't for mine).

So the only options that are left to us, are:

- put up with the difficulties your child is experiencing, and try to limit the damage being done to their wellbeing

- put up with being bullied / shut down as a parent by your child's school

- or leave, in the hope that another school will be better

But even this doesn't really work, especially when the whole system of mainstream school, the very power-balance itself, is 100% stacked against SEND families.
At one point, LongRoadDad and I had steered Big Bruv through 4 school settings in as many years. Little Sis is now in her 4th setting, after being basically forced out of her 1st, 2nd and 3rd.

So it's not like we haven't tried the "exit" option ourselves..!

© The Long Road / Long Road SENDMum

In an education system where no-one wants to (or is able to) "pick up the tab" and really engage with our kids' SEND needs, it's my family's lived experience that moving mainstream schools just moves the problem - the problem being that mainstream schools **do not want to have to adapt in order to meet our kids' needs.**

Because they do not see them.

And Local Authorities do not want to see them either - even though The Law tells Local Authorities it is they who are ultimately responsible for meeting our children's SEND needs, and the Law is actually really clear:

- Mainstream schools should <u>not</u> think it's OK to view meeting Special Educational Needs as if it is optional: **it is not**

- Schools should <u>not</u> think it's OK to ignore a child's diagnosis or what's in a child's care plan - whether that's

25

an Additional Needs Plan, a My Support Plan, or an EHCP: **it is not**

- <u>No</u> SEND child or family should be pushed so far by a school, that they feel the only option left to them is to leave

- And no SEND family should have to watch a school and/or Local Authority <u>wilfully</u> *and* <u>knowingly</u> abdicate their lawful duty to a child

But that is what's happening.

So, in this book I'm going to explore why it's happening, how it's happening, and exactly what the professionals ought to be doing – but far too often are not.

© The Long Road

Anyone Can Be A SEND Parent

SEND stands for **Special Educational Needs and Disabilities.** It's very important to note that although I use the term SEND as a catch-all for our children and their needs throughout this book, Special Educational Needs & Disabilities are not necessarily the same thing:

- A child can have Special Educational Needs, without having a disability
- And a child can have a disability, without having Special Educational Needs

Either way, anyone can be - or can become - a SEND parent.

I know what many people will be thinking when they read that sentence .. "How does that even work? How could anyone be a parent to a Special Needs and/or Disabled child and not know it?!"

Well, if it makes you feel any better, LongRoadDad and I didn't know. Not for a very long time.

It's all to do with what Special Educational Needs & Disabilities look like to the wider world. It also has a lot to do with why I've titled this book "We Are Not Seeing It": that single phrase haunts far too many SEND parents' lives on a pretty much daily basis.

Sometimes, it's really obvious from birth that a child has SEND .. And sometimes it's really, really not!

The world is getting much better at understanding the visible type of SEND life; people generally tend these days to be both sympathetic and supportive of kids with Downs, or cerebral palsy or muscular dystrophy and other types of visible disability, kids who need mobility aids or visual aids or hearing aids - mostly because people can *see* the child's difficulties.

But what about the things the wider world cannot so easily see?

What about children who are struggling with mental health issues: depression, anxiety, disordered eating, or self harm? Well, mental health difficulties that have a long-lasting effect on a person's day to day life are classed as a disability under the Equality Act 2010: **that makes you a SEND parent.**

Type 1 Childhood Diabetes? Ehlers Danlos Syndrome? Again, these are conditions considered as disabilities under the Equality Act 2010. So is a temporary disability. Not something small like a broken leg, I'm talking about big, life-changing stuff like receiving treatment for cancer. **That would make you a SEND parent.**

What about the so-called "Hidden Disabilities" (now more often referred to as "Invisible Disabilities"), like the ones my children have? Things like ADHD. Dyspraxia. Sensory Processing Disorder. Autism.

Autism is considered by the medical profession to be a Multifactorial Disorder*, just like Spina Bifida.
But our son (Big Bruv) was about 7 years old before it even occurred to us that he was struggling so much in school because he's autistic.
(* - Source: https://www.nature.com/articles/s41467-021-25487-6)

As for ADHD, which is a Specific Learning Difficulty? It never even crossed our minds.
We were SEND parents, and we didn't even know it!

Big Bruv's reality never occurred to us, because Big Bruv masks. And it was not his school that brought that fact to our attention: we had to work it out for ourselves.

Big Bruv's nursery never saw his needs.
His first school refused to accept he might be struggling (or that autism might be a possibility).
And so did the second school he went to.
And the third.

He was just "quirky".
He was being a bit "naughty".
He was inattentive.
He had terrible handwriting.
He couldn't stay on task.
As one primary school Head Teacher described him, he was "a very unusual child".
But in their expert opinion, it wasn't anything else.

Your child is not masking in school. We are not seeing it.

Idiot...

© The Long Road.

You see, the nursery and the school were looking for what they thought autism *ought* to look like.

- Repetitive behaviours
- No eye contact
- Obsessively putting things in rows
- Social difficulties
- Meltdowns

All those "classic" signs that films like Rain Man (compounded by a huge dearth of training), told teachers what autism is "supposed" to look like.

Instead, in Big Bruv they were dealing with a bright, articulate, expressive and communicative child with oodles of ideas and very few obviously repetitive behaviours. A young man who gave loads of eye contact, and who was happy to make and have friends. (ps. For the record, eye contact is not a reliable indicator of autism and I wish so-called professionals would stop pretending it is!)

As for his ADHD traits, again, teachers were looking for the "classic" signs:
- Inattentiveness
- "Behavioural issues"
- Uncontrolled hyperactivity / tics / fidgeting
- Shouting or hitting
- Throwing furniture or running out of school

Instead, in Big Bruv they had a child who often could sit at a desk - even though he clearly found it very difficult. A child who could hyper-focus (a genuine ADHD trait) when he was really interested in something, but which made it really difficult to transition from one task to another (which was then interpreted as laziness and/or defiance). They were also dealing with a child who didn't throw massive wobbles, shout, swear, bounce off the walls, hit things/other kids, run out of school, or have other "behavioural issues".

But just because they couldn't see Big Bruv's difficulties didn't mean those difficulties were not there.
The school was dealing with a child whose school-related distress and trauma were growing by the day - but distress and trauma that he was comprehensively masking and internalising, to the very best of his ability, while he was in school. Until he couldn't anymore.

As a parent who was dealing with the aftermath of Big Bruv's day in school on an increasingly regular basis, and who was relying on these professional people for help and guidance, I couldn't help but ask myself:

"If that Head Teacher of some 20+ years experience, who has probably taught thousands of children in their career, thinks Big Bruv is "unusual" .. but at the same time is telling me he is "fine" in school (when he clearly isn't "fine" in school at all..!) then what on earth is going on?"

It was <u>only</u> when we, as his parents, began to look at Big Bruv's school experience through the lens of autism, that the picture began to make a little bit of sense.

Soon after we had the realisation that our son was probably autistic, we also came to see our daughter (Little Sis) was struggling every bit as much as her brother. But she was masking her difficulties *even more* comprehensively, so they were *even harder* to see (We'll come to masking and different presentations later).
Yet trying to convince their teachers, or the medical professionals around them..?
Oh my goodness, no LongRoadMum, that can't be right!
You're "just" mum.
What on earth do you know in the face of our years of training and expertise?
Don't be so silly and unreasonable. If there is something "wrong" with your children, and your children are struggling to fit into the education system, or just society in general, then it can't possibly be an "Invisible Disability"!

"Perhaps your son just needs to learn to sit still more and practise harder with his handwriting?"

"Perhaps your daughter needs to not be so aloof?" (yes, that is a direct quote from one of Little Sis's teachers..) **"Then she won't get singled out and be picked on by the other girls."**

Whatever the case, we are the experts.
If there was something to see, we would have seen it.
And we don't.

It must be a behavioural or a parenting problem.
It must be yours, or your child's fault.
If your child only explodes at home, it must be a <u>home</u> problem.

And that's how my family's journey into the SEND world began - a journey filled with suspicion, punishment, blame and guilt, **all of which were being piled on us and made a hundred times worse by our kids' school.**

How had we not realised we had, not one but TWO autistic kids? And how hard had this been for our children?!
Had we accidentally made it worse by using all those well-worn parenting ideas like punishment and reward, or "letting them cry it out" because they're "just trying to get their own way"?
Had we then made things even worse by nodding along whenever teachers told us our kids needed to develop more "resilience", and gave us their "expert" opinions?   Opinions we were now beginning to see were completely wrong?

More to the point, if these people really _are_ the professionals, why did no-one - nursery staff, Early Years practitioners, primary school TAs, teachers, heads or governors - see our children's SEND before us?

Why did that Head Teacher describe our son as "unusual" .. but then do literally nothing to help us work out why?

Once we had realised the road we were travelling, there were no professionals standing ready to point the way for us. They were far more likely to point the finger of blame - and still are all these years later.

Because my kids are so adept at masking their needs, and because their presentations are inward, rather than outward, **there was, and still is, nothing the wider world can see, to help them understand that both Big Bruv and Little Sis have Special Educational Needs and invisible disabilities:**
- Autism (Both)
- ADHD (Big Bruv)
- Dysgraphia (Both)
- Hypermobility (Both)
- Sensory integration issues (Both)

- Developmental Co-Ordination Disorder / Dyspraxia (Little Sis)
- All of which have led to, and been compounded by, episodes of crippling anxiety, and self esteem that's often collapsed through the floor

These are conditions and disabilities that entitle my kids to every bit as much help and support and empathy and understanding as any other need or disability ~ but support, help and understanding that we have had to (and continue to have to) fight tooth and nail to get for them.

Why This Matters for SEND Families ...

- My kids are just like yours: wonderful young people, with a vast well of talent and ability and creativity and artistry and science and music and fun and humour and determination and hundreds of other fabulous things to offer the world, and **who are just as entitled to be in school as any other child.** And who also happen to have invisible Special Educational Needs & Disabilities.

- The education system in its current form is not working for SEND families: it is <u>forcing</u> us to make an impossible choice:
    - Fight a system that is 100% stacked against you
    - Or leave

What is School For, And Why Do We Send Our Kids There?

It's a simple question .. but it's also a very complex one.

As a parent, my view of school when my children were very young was as follows:

- I went to school
- All kids go to school; kids going to school is "normal"
- The Law says I have to send them to school*. There isn't any other way to do it.
  (* - not quite the case. More about this later)
- School is about education, and children need a formal education
- School also lets my children make friends with kids their own age, and that's really important for them
- School teaches my children valuable life skills - like how to co-operate with others, how to be cared for by people other than us (their parents).
- They'll learn social skills, and become more independent at school; all of these things are really important too
- One (or both) of us might be able to re-establish a career, once the children start school
- Schools know what they are doing, and how best to educate and care for kids. They are the trained professionals. They will look after my child
- All in all, going to school is A Good Thing

If I could go back now and speak to the me who thought all those things all those years ago, we'd probably have a very different conversation! But that was then. As the saying goes, "You don't know what you don't know". And LongRoadDad and I really did <u>not</u> know what we were letting ourselves or our children in for.

That said, even back then, I knew in my heart that what parents **absolutely do not** send their children to school for is:

- For our child not to receive a suitable education - i.e. one that meets their needs and that they can access successfully
- For them to be bullied, singled out or socially isolated - by their peers *and/or their teachers*
- If things go wrong, for them (and us) to be gaslighted, shamed or blamed
- For our child to have their mental health and wellbeing utterly destroyed
- For them to end up so mentally broken and emotionally traumatised, they might not be able to attend school any more at all

Those last points seem like they go without saying, right? Yes, of course! As we've already established, the main train of thought is that going to school is "A Good Thing", and that "Teachers Are Professionals" - they know what they are doing. Of course none of the other things could possibly happen!

And that's what LongRoadDad and I thought too.

So, just like thousands and thousands of children every September, off my children went - first to a local nursery, and then on to Reception class at our local school.

Let's remember, at this time, we did not know either of our children were autistic or ADHD or anything. There was **nothing** to make us suspect that their journey through the school system would be anything other than "normal" (whatever that actually means).

Looking back, I can now see things actually started to go wrong for Big Bruv pretty early – we just didn't know it. But we'll come to that in more detail later. For now, let's continue with our exploration of what mainstream schools are for, how they came to exist in their current form, why they operate the way they do - and why that matters so much for SEND families.

19th Century Values in 21st Century Education

Even today, people still half-jokingly refer to "The Three R's" ("Reading, 'Riting, 'Rithmatic") that were the foundations of 19th century ideas about education.

We can see them being role-played in the Victorian school room of every Living History museum up and down the country - and as parents we all squirm a bit, and give a little chuckle of recognition as the cosplaying school ma'am or master struts up and down the wooden benches, barking orders at us and threatening some unfortunate grown-up with "the cane".

Why do we recognise this method of education?
Because those "Three R's", and the way they were delivered, have never actually left the classroom.
What we are cosplaying in a living history museum is not *that* different to what our own school experiences were like. And even now in the 21st century, our kids still recognise these things too, because school education in the UK still holds on to a lot of its 19th century history. For example, rote learning of things like times tables is still very much a requirement. Both SATS and GCSEs require a fixed set of "learnings" to be absolutely hammered into kids' brains, in order for them to pass those tests.

So let's explore that history a little more.

The majority of state schooling in the UK finds its very earliest roots in the 18th and 19th centuries, when charitable organisations, churches, Sunday Schools, and so-called "Ragged Schools" for the very poorest children, began to develop. Many of the ideas employed in these very earliest schools were the basis for modern concepts of primary and secondary education.

"The Sandon Act (1876), for the first-time compelled parents to send their sons/daughters to school between the ages 5-10. This was followed by the Elementary Education Act (1880) that enforced school boards to enforce compulsory school attendance from 5-10 years old. Despite this act, children deemed to have met the required standards could still be employed before the age of ten, with poorer parents often keen that they do so to bring an income into the household."

(Source: https://www.designtechnology.org.uk/news/150-years-of-state-education-a-time-to-reflect/)

For me, there are two very important points in that paragraph:

- the requirement of **enforced, compulsory attendance**, and
- that the goal of education / the measure of success of education was **the employability of children**

Not the quality or suitability of the education received, not the wellbeing of the child, nor their maturity, readiness or ability to start or leave school .. but their employability

Obviously there have been many more pieces of education legislation since the 1876 Sandon Act. But it is worth reiterating that the purpose of the earliest forms of school education was not to create well-rounded human beings, but to provide **proficient and compliant employees** to 19th century factory owners, the merchants and administrators of the British Empire, the armed forces and so on. These were the engines of the vast wealth of Britain well into the middle of the 20th century. And they needed, not thinkers, or creative minds, or artists or poets - or indeed children with Special Educational Needs.

They required employees who were:
- Literate
- Numerate
- Punctual
- Sober
- Able to follow instructions from those in authority

Those historical "measures of success" - the future employability of children - still sit at the heart of every single child's mainstream school experience in the UK to this day.

Why This Matters for SEND Families:

- "The "Sandon Act" (Act of 1876) imposed a legal duty on parents to ensure that their children **were educated**."

    o This requirement still lives on in the Education Act 1996

- "The Elementary Education Act 1880 (the "Mundella Act") required **school boards to enforce compulsory attendance** from 5 to 10 years"

    o This requirement <u>does not</u> live on in the Education Act 1996

- **Section 7 of the Education Act** 1996 states (with my emphasis) that:

    o The parent of every child of compulsory school age shall cause him* to receive **efficient full-time education suitable**

        ▪ (a) to his* age, ability and aptitude, and
        ▪ (b) to any special educational needs he* may have,
        ▪ **either by regular attendance at school** <u>or</u> <u>otherwise</u>

- **Section 19(6) of the Education Act 1996** confirms that:

    o "Suitable" means to provide "efficient education, suitable to his* age, ability and aptitude and any special educational needs he may have"

(* - please note this is not a typo: it is the actual wording in the legislation. So please don't write in - I didn't choose the pronouns. Thanks!)

- So whilst it is compulsory for a child to **receive education** once they reach statutory school age, doing so full time **at a school is actually not compulsory**
  - In other words, school attendance is not necessarily the "default setting" under the law. But that is a very well-kept secret!

(Source: DfE Elective Home Education Departmental Guidance For Parents, April 2019 - https://assets.publishing.service.gov.uk/media/5ca21e22e5274a77d9d26feb/ EHE_guidance_for_parentsafterconsultationv2.2.pdf)

As I've already said, I'm not going to take a deep dive into either EHE or Flexischooling in this book - there are lots of excellent authors who have already done that. All I will say is, in my experience at least:

- No-one in government, or at council level, or in a school, ever tells the majority of parents, before our children start school, that we have a right to choose Elective Home Education, and/or Flexischooling, if we want to

- And to many of us, the idea of anything other than mainstream school seems so utterly unusual/so far from "the norm", that most of us would never consider it as our first choice anyway – because we don't know our kids might need it

Violence = Compliance

How did the early school system ensure the employees it was churning out met all the expectations of what a "good" employee should be? Largely, it did it through rote learning, competition, shame and some often quite violent punishment.

We all know that children in Victorian schools, and right through to the 20th century, would be routinely punished or shamed with such draconian methods as the "dunce cap", "the naughty corner", the belt, the slipper, the strap, the tawse, or the cane.

Left-handed children were routinely shamed, punished, hit, or had their left hand physically restrained, to teach them to write "the correct way".

It was not unusual for disruptive children (most likely boys, but also some girls) to be sent to Industrial Schools, Reform Schools, Approved Schools or "Borstal". (Source: www.childrenshomes.org.uk/BI).

Disruptive or dysregulated girls were highly likely to be institutionalised in mental hospitals or asylums, with that hideous catch-all (and quack) diagnosis of "Hysteria".

All of us have older relatives who can tell us real-life stories of the violence that was metered out against children in schools "back in the day". For example, in the early 1950s LongRoadGrandad attended a religious school where it was very common for boys to be beaten with canes or the slipper, just because the child had dared to answer back, "mess around", the Master was having a bad day and/or felt like it.

One of the Masters at LongRoadGrandad's school even gave his cane a pet name and would walk around the classroom with it, taking random aim at a misplaced hand on a desk or a child's back - again, just because he felt like it.

But "back in the day" is not as far back as we might like to think.

- I had a primary school RE teacher who was well known for punching children in the back if they misbehaved in her class

- Another of my primary school teachers kept a cane in her classroom. Even though she wasn't allowed to use it, she still liked the effect just having it on view, had on the children in her class: i.e. Fear

- Long Road Dad and I frequently saw heavy blackboard rubbers being launched by teachers at unruly kids - who were usually, but not always exclusively, boys.

For anyone too young to remember even so much as a blackboard (!) never mind the rubber that went with it, these items were an essential piece of kit in every classroom during mine and LongRoadDad's childhood. They were made of solid wood with a piece of felt attached. They weighed a few hundred grammes at least. As I'm sure you can imagine, a piece of solid wood weighing a quarter of a kilo could be capable of inflicting a pretty nasty blow, if it was thrown at a child with any kind of force .. But who on earth would do such a thing?!

Well, mine and LongRoadDad's teachers did it, pretty much on a daily basis.

The teachers who used this method of classroom control were surprisingly good at split-second aiming of their weapon of choice directly at a child's head:

- If a blackboard rubber got you on the back of the head or the temple, not much tended to happen. Everyone would point and laugh, and the class would carry on

- If the blackboard rubber hit you straight in the face (as sometimes happened), you might get sent to see the school nurse to clean up any blood

- But whatever the case, everyone in charge was usually in agreement: the injured child "deserved it", and everyone got on with their day

That wasn't in the 19th century, or even the 1950s. It was in the 1980s.

Would it surprise you to learn that actual corporal punishment in UK schools was only successfully challenged by parents Grace Campbell and Jane Cosans, when they took their case to the European Court of Human Rights in 1982?
(Ref:
http://news.bbc.co.uk/onthisday/hi/dates/stories/february/25/newsid_251600 0/2516621.stm)

And that corporal punishment was ultimately abolished in UK state schools only as late as 1986?

Or that the same ban was not extended to fee-paying/private schools until March 1998?

"My advice to members is: carry on caning" –

David Hart, teachers' union, 1982

(Source:
http://news.bbc.co.uk/onthisday/hi/dates/stories/february/25/newsid_2516000/25 16621.stm)

What I find really telling here is that no-one in the school system itself saw fit to challenge the corporal punishment taking place in schools: **it was parents who had to challenge the practice of routine physical violence against their children**, and get it removed from the classroom.

Let's also consider another very important point: The majority of the children who were on the receiving end of these draconian punishments, physical beatings and routine shaming, were not just "acting up" for the fun of it. I'd make an educated guess the majority of them were probably children with what we would now recognise as Special Educational Needs and/or Disabilities: things like autism, ADHD, PDA, sensory difficulties, dyslexia, dysgraphia and so on.

Conditions which are largely still as poorly recognised or understood by many teachers today, as they were in the 1980s when corporal punishment was still legal.

Why This Matters To SEND Families:

- **The Children & Families Act 2014*** contains the legal rights to ensure children with Special Educational Needs receive the educational provision required as a result of their needs

  (* - The Children & Families Act 2014 applies in England. Other parts of the UK may have different legislation in force)

- **The Equality Act 2010** means it is <u>unlawful</u> to discriminate against disabled pupils in school - for example, by not making "reasonable adjustments" for a child's SEND - *whether they have a diagnosis or not*

  But ...

- **Punishment is built into the DNA of the UK school system**: Children's wellbeing, their emotions, or the routine practice of adapting to special needs/disabilities, is *not*

- When corporal punishment was outlawed in schools, there was no attempt to review or reform the thinking about school discipline:

  - Ideas about discipline remained the much same - i.e. "naughty kids need (and deserve) punishment"

○ The methods of punishment in schools may have stopped being corporal, but that doesn't mean the violence has gone away:

  ▪ The violence is often harder to see because now, it's usually psychological (more on that later)
  ▪ And physical violence has not actually gone away - especially not for SEND kids (more on that later, too).

- Discipline policies in schools **disproportionately** affect Special Educational Needs and/or Disabled kids

  ○ Everything a child does that is not within a set criteria of "good behaviour", is still framed as "bad behaviour" which needs to be controlled or punished

    ▪ I call this "Command and Control" and I'll come back to it many times, because it has *such* a huge influence on children's experiences in school.

  ○ "Behaviour" is *never* seen as a form of communication; nor is "bad", "disruptive" or "difficult" behaviour ever seen as a sign of distress and/or unmet need

  ○ A child with additional or special educational needs (whether diagnosed or not) **is far more likely to receive sanctions, punishments, "demerits", detentions and routine shaming** than their non-SEND peers

Look at any modern school discipline policy **through a lens of Special Needs and Disabilities**, and behaviour being a form of communication (instead of seeing everything as good old fashioned "bad behaviour") and you will see a lot that will horrify you.

Elements of the Education Act 2011 - particularly the sections regarding Discipline - will also provide a lot of info that will horrify you. I'll come back to this very important point later, where we'll explore discipline methods, take a deeper dive into "Command and Control", and see how the Education Act 2011 fundamentally changed the balance of power between families and schools.

For now though, let's continue to explore what parents are actually signing up for, and who with, when they send their child into mainstream education.

"The Social Contract"

Educators and previous Governments have liked to make a big deal about the "social contract" that's meant to exist between home and school. They have also liked to talk a lot about parents "breaking" that social contract by not sending our children to school - no matter how distressed or traumatised our children might be when, for the sake of their mental health and wellbeing, we make the momentous decision to stop sending them to school.

Well, if we and our children are entering into a "contract" when we send our kids off to Reception class at the age of 4 or 5, surely parents should be allowed to know what the terms of that "contract" actually are? And who will be carrying out that "contract"? (Especially if, as we've already seen, it's not actually *legally required* for us to send our kiddo to school in the first place!).

I'd like to think so. So let's explore this "social contract" in more detail.

There are 5 very important elements that parents are never, in my experience at least, made aware of when our children start school, but which form a very large part of what the "social contract" between families and schools actually is:

- "In Loco Parentis"
- The role of Teaching Assistants
- The Early Years Foundation Stage
- Teacher's Standards
- Quality First Teaching

These last 3 documents are particularly important because they set out what the role and expectations of a teacher / education professional are. We'll look at them in more detail shortly.

Let's start with a large part of the "social contract" parents enter into when they leave their child at the classroom door - but one I would bet 99.9% of parents are utterly unaware of: that a teacher, a TA, and a school as a whole, becomes "*In loco parentis*" to the children in their care.

"In Loco Parentis": What Does It Actually Mean?

From https://www.lawandparents.co.uk/: "You may have heard the phrase 'in loco parentis' many times before, but did you know that it actually has legal significance when it comes to looking after other people's children – either on a casual or educational basis. 'In loco parentis' is Latin for 'instead of a parent' and in English law it applies in several circumstances.

Examples Of The Duty Of Care
When you leave your child at the school gates you are in effect agreeing to allow the teachers and other staff at the school to act 'in loco parentis'. You also act in loco parentis when your child's friends come to stay, or if you take your children and other people's children on a trip to a local park. Babysitters, childminders, nursery assistants, crèche supervisors and holiday camp supervisors also assume a duty of care during the course of their employment.

Relevant Legislation
So what does this legal definition actually mean in practical terms? There are two statutory provisions that relate to the role of teachers

acting in loco parentis: first, the Children Act 1989 provides that teachers have a duty of care towards the children under their supervision, as well as promoting the safety and welfare of the children in their care. The level of this duty of care is measured as being that of a 'reasonable parent.'

Let's just unpick that for a moment.
It would be utterly remiss of a parent not to vet their babysitter or child-minder before leaving their child with them, even for an hour.

Yet we are expected (under the guise of it being "lawfully required") to deliver and entrust our child into the care of their teacher and any TAs at a school, often never having met these people so much as once - and with no opportunity to do so until many weeks into the term.

There are no other relationships in a child's life that parents have so little input into, or so little control over, than who is going to be our child's teacher and/or TA.

Yet from day 1, these people are "in loco parentis" for our child. And we know literally nothing about them!

At the same time, on the first day of term - and save for perhaps some handover notes written by another teacher or a child's pre-school/childminder - the teacher and any TAs know just about nothing, not just about our child, but also the 30 or so other children in their care.

These are people who are now responsible for our child for up to 6 hours a day, 5 days a week.

On the first day of school, our child will be lucky to have met their teacher any more than 2 or 3 times at a transition day or two.
They have probably never met the TAs at all.
And yet the child is expected to unquestioningly trust these people from day one, and do exactly what the teacher and the TAs say from day one .. **and feel happy, safe and secure about it.**

Now, I am not saying that parents should be demanding to have absolute control over who their child's teacher or TA is; that would be completely unworkable. If we are agreeing to send our child into school, rather than to electively home educate them, use EOTAS, flexischool or hire our own tutor, then we must also accept that we have to take a leap of faith and trust the teacher(s) or TAs assigned to our child have the professional competence, care and ability to do the job they are paid to do.

"In loco parentis" is an act of faith.

"The social contract" is an act of faith.

Believing the teacher and TAs in charge of your child are sufficiently qualified and capable, not just to educate, but to also take reasonable care of your child, is an act of faith.

And for the majority of the time, for many children, that arrangement *does* work.

But that statement comes with a caveat: **Sometimes it doesn't work.**

Why This Matters To SEND Families:

- Teachers and TAs have a duty of care towards the children under their supervision
  - The level of this duty of care is measured as being that of a 'reasonable parent.'

  - Teachers/educators spend so much time with the children they teach, many become used to their role - and their judgement about a child - going unquestioned

  - **But teachers and TAs are not the child's parents. We are.** And no matter how much time our kids spend in school, we still know our children better than anyone!

Teaching Assistants

The role of a Teaching Assistant is a crucial part of the professional mix in a school. As class sizes grow ever larger, the input of a TA becomes all the more important: one teacher simply cannot have eyes on every single child under their care, every minute of the day.

Teaching Assistants have a set of Professional Standards which they should adhere to. Crucially though, and unlike the mandatory (i.e. lawfully binding) Teacher's Standards, which we'll cover shortly:

> "The TA standards are non-mandatory and non-statutory, but they sit alongside the statutory standards for teachers and headteachers. They help to define the role and purpose of TAs to ensure that schools can maximise the educational value and contribution of adults working with pupils.
> (Source: https://maximisingtas.co.uk/resources/professional-standards-for-teaching-assistants.php#:~:text=The%20TA%20standards%20are%20non,of%20adults%20working%20with%20pupils.)

Good TAs are able to be fabulous advocates − and a genuine potential "early warning system" - for SEND kids in their earliest days at school.

TAs could be the ones who flag up where a child is having difficulties that might need further investigation:

- Perhaps a child is reading out loud way above their expected age range, but is clearly struggling with processing and understanding the things they are reading

- Maybe a child needs instructions or questions reading out to them, because they can't zone in on the teacher speaking from the front, they struggle to copy from the board, or they can't grasp the meaning of the words on their worksheet

- Perhaps a child is having trouble getting their "b" and "d" the right way round

- Perhaps a child has an unconventional way of holding their pencil, and writing is clearly difficult/is not progressing as much as expected

○ Maybe the child is pressing so hard on the paper their fingers are hurting, but they can't do it any other way

○ Maybe they cannot keep their writing on the lines, or ever remember to put a "finger space" between words. Maybe punctuation just doesn't happen, no matter how many reminders are given.

• Maybe a child tends to "zone out" a lot, or needs to fidget and move, no matter how many times in the school day they are reminded not to

All these things could be signs of an unrecognised SEND need. And TAs could be a really effective "early warning system", simply because they spend more time at the desk or learning table, in very close contact with the children, than one classroom teacher is ever able to.

Yet crucially, Teaching Assistants can be recruited, and start in post, having received no SEND training whatsoever. This is a problem. If TAs:

• Have no idea of what an early presentation of unmet Special Educational Need looks like

• Have no real understanding of masking and what that looks like either - and neither does the classroom teacher or the SENCO

• Must defer to the knowledge, judgement and seniority of the classroom teacher

And everything that happens in class is framed as "good behaviour" or "bad behaviour" or even "laziness" / "lack of effort" on the child's part .. then the chance for a TA to flag up any potential problems, or for professionals to intervene early, will all too often be missed.

Why This Matters for SEND Families:

- Unlike Teacher's Standards (which we'll look at later), Teaching Assistant's Standards are non-mandatory and non-statutory

    ○ Their role is not governed to the same professional standards as that of a teacher
    ○ and a TA is not at the same professional level/rank as a teacher

- A TA's role is hugely important in the classroom (And due to shortages, many actually teach classes!)

- Teaching Assistants are usually in the closest contact with children – especially SEND children - throughout the school day

- **Yet Teaching Assistants can be recruited, and start in post, having received no SEND training whatsoever**

- The teacher is the TA's professional superior

    ○ Even if a TA has concerns about a child, teachers do not have to listen to, or accept, the views of Teaching Assistants

- The relationship a SEND child has with a Teaching Assistant can be absolutely critical to that child's success:

    ○ A good TA, who really cares about and understands the child and their needs, has the power to determine a child's whole future at a school

    ○ The opposite is also true: A poorly-trained or poorly supervised TA (or one who is "Not Seeing It" and so frames unmet need as "behaviour")

also has the power to determine a child's whole future at a school

---

The Early Years Foundation Stage Framework

The EYFSF (formerly called the Early Years Framework) was updated in January 2024. You can read the EYFSF here: https://www.gov.uk/government/publications/early-years-foundation-stage-framework--2

This document:

> " … is for all group and school-based early years providers in England (including maintained schools; non-maintained schools; independent schools; free schools; and academies) and all group-based providers on the Early Years Register."

In points 2 to 4 of its Introduction, the EYFSF says:

> 2. The EYFS sets the standards that all early years providers must meet to ensure that children learn and develop well and are kept healthy and safe. It promotes teaching and learning to ensure children's 'school readiness' and gives children the right foundation for good future progress through school and life.

> 3. The EYFS is about what children learn, as well as how they learn. Effective practice is a mix of different approaches. Children learn through play, by adults modelling, by observing each other and through adult-guided learning.

> 4. The EYFS seeks to provide:
> • Quality and consistency in all early years settings, so that every child makes good progress, and no child gets left behind.
> • A secure foundation through planning for the learning and development of each individual child, and assessing and reviewing what they have learned regularly.

• Partnership working between practitioners and with parents and/or carers.
• Equality of opportunity and anti-discriminatory practice, ensuring that every child is included and supported.

Additionally:

"The Early Years Foundation Stage (EYFS) **statutory** framework is **mandatory** for all early years settings. It sets the standards that all early years providers must meet to ensure that children learn and develop well and are kept health and safe."

So we can see the EYFS Framework lays out a set of very important standards, which *all* Early Years providers should know, and should be adhering to **by law**, from day 1.

It aims to ensure that
• all children get the very best start in their school life
• every child should be supported
• no child should be discriminated against
• every child makes good progress
• no child gets left behind

And it applies to everyone from schools to nurseries, and even to childminders.

Additionally, the SEND Code of Practice Paragraph 5.36 notes:

"It is particularly important in the early years that there is no delay in making any necessary special educational provision".

So far so good then!

Why This Matters For SEND Families:

In theory, no child with Special Educational Needs should ever fall through the cracks:

- The Early Years Foundation Stage Framework is designed and intended to make sure no child is left behind in their education, even from the very earliest days

and

- The SEND Code of Practice also tells Early Years settings what they should be doing to help even the youngest child

- The EYFSF is **statutory** and **mandatory**. It is lawfully required, and it is <u>not</u> optional

so

- Even though the Teaching Assistant's Standards are neither mandatory nor statutory, **the EYFSF is** (and so are Teacher's Standards - more on those in a second)

- The provisions in the EYFSF *should* mean that <u>every</u> child with Special Educational Needs has those emerging needs recognised in an Early Years setting

---

Teacher's Standards

Teacher's Standards "were introduced on 1 September 2012 to set a clear baseline of expectations for the professional practice and conduct of teachers."
(Source: https://www.gov.uk/government/publications/teachers-standards)

Teacher's Standards set out very clearly the obligations and expectations that <u>every</u> teacher has to adhere to, from the moment they have finished their training and entered their first teaching post, right through to the end of their teaching career. And - unlike the Teaching Assistant's Standards - they are both **mandatory** and **statutory**.

That means they are lawfully binding.

You can see an overview of the Teacher's Standards on the GOV.UK website. They are definitely worth reading, because they form a really important part of the Social Contract parents enter into when we send our child off to school – but again, no-one <u>ever</u> mentions them to parents.

I particularly want to mention Teacher's Standard #5, which places the following professional expectation (or Standard) on <u>all</u> teachers:

5: Adapt teaching to respond to the strengths and needs of all pupils
- know when and how to differentiate appropriately, using approaches which enable pupils to be taught effectively
- have a secure understanding of how a range of factors can inhibit pupils' ability to learn, and how best to overcome these
- demonstrate an awareness of the physical, social and intellectual development of children, and know how to adapt teaching to support pupils' education at different stages of development
- have a clear understanding of the needs of all pupils, including those with special educational needs; those of high ability; those with English as an additional language; those with disabilities; and be able to use and evaluate distinctive teaching approaches to engage and support them.

Again, so far so good: The standards and expectations being placed upon the people who are working with, caring for and educating our children are all very clear, and absolutely what we, as parents, should expect.

In addition to the Teacher's Standards, there are also the Headteacher's Standards.
(https://www.gov.uk/government/publications/national-standards-of-excellence-for-headteachers/headteachers-standards-2020)

Headteacher's Standards were updated in 2020 and sit alongside the Teacher's Standards. To quote from gov.uk:

"Headteachers, like other teachers, are expected to meet the teachers' standards. The headteachers' standards articulate how headteachers can meet both the additional responsibilities of headship and the requirements of the teachers' standards.

The first section of the headteachers' standards outlines the ethics and professional conduct expected of headteachers. This is developed from part 2 of the teachers' standards. As such, they consist of statements that define the behaviour and attitudes which should be expected of headteachers."

Additionally:

"Headteachers are leading professionals and role models for the communities they serve. Their leadership is a significant factor in ensuring high quality teaching and achievement in schools and a positive and enriching experience of education for pupils. Together with those responsible for governance, they are custodians of the nation's schools.

Parents and the wider public rightly hold high expectations of headteachers, given their influential position leading the teaching profession and on the young people who are their responsibility. The headteachers' standards set out how headteachers meet these high expectations. The standards are an important benchmark not only for headteachers and those who hold headteachers to account, but also for those who train and develop school leaders."

Interestingly, the Headteacher's Standards are <u>not</u> statutory. So although Headteachers must still adhere to the Teacher's Standards (because those are statutory and mandatory), that disconnect between Teacher's Standards **and Headteacher's Standards** leaves room for interpretation by individual Heads about exactly how they use their influence, how they act as role models, and what their own definition of "high quality teaching" might look like.

Above all though, let's remember that everyone who works in the education sector is a public servant – so the Nolan Principles of Public Life apply to everything they do. Those principles are:

○ Selflessness, Integrity, Objectivity, Accountability, Honesty, Openness and Leadership (Source: https://www.gov.uk/government/publications/the-7-principles-of-public-life/the-7-principles-of-public-life--2)

Why This Matters For SEND Families:

- As public servants, teachers and heads are expected to uphold the Nolan Principles of Public Life

- Teacher's Standards mean there is a **lawful** requirement placed upon all teachers to

    - adapt teaching to the needs of all pupils
    - to understand what those needs may be
    - and to understand and work within the lawful frameworks required of teachers

    - But Headteacher's Standards do not align 100% with the Teacher's Standards, and so are open to interpretation by individual Headteachers

- In theory, Teacher's Standards and the EYFSF should ensure that *no* child passes through:

    - the Early Years Foundation Stage Framework
    - or the care of a teacher who is following all Teacher's Standards
    - without any Special Educational Needs being spotted/the right interventions being put in place

BUT..

- Neither The EYFSF, nor Teacher's Standards, say anything about **identifying a child with a disability**. And neither do the Headteacher's Standards.

- In other words, there is an expectation that

  o A disabled child will be identified to the teacher by someone, somewhere

  and/or

  o The child's disability needs are being met by some means, by someone, somewhere

- So, if no-one knows the child has a disability (e.g. like no-one saw that Big Bruv and Little Sis were autistic)

  o **no-one in a school is compelled to actively look for an invisible disability like autism**

    ▪ Even though autistic kids have a disability
    ▪ and, because of their disability, they <u>also</u> <u>have Special Educational Needs</u>

Quality First Teaching

I've often been told by schools that "All teachers are teachers of SEND, because of Quality First Teaching" / QFT.

In theory, that statement should be correct that because QFT has 3 "Waves", or levels:

- **Wave 1** of QFT sets out what is expected to be achievable for the majority of children in a mainstream setting

- **Wave 2** is the next step of support – for example if a child has been identified as struggling in class.

- **Wave 3** is the highest level of support / intervention that a child may need. (Children who need Wave 3 will almost undoubtedly have Special Educational Needs.)

So, what can we find out about Wave 1 of QFT? Here's a summary from Optimus Education:
(Source: https://my.optimus-education.com/what-quality-first-teaching-and-why-it-important)

"Quality first teaching is a term that is often used within education. It originated in a 2008 Department for Children, Schools and Families (DCSF) policy document called 'Personalised Learning – A practical guide'.

QFT emphasises the importance of relationships between the classroom teacher and pupils, and encourages higher expectations through higher levels of support for all pupils.

In the document, the DCSF asserted that QFT:

'… demands 100% participation from the pupils, and sets high and realistic challenges. It does not 'spoon feed', it is challenging and demanding; it expects pupils to be able to articulate their ideas, understanding and thinking by actively promoting pupil talk.' (page 10)

One of the biggest changes in education in the last 15 years has been the shift towards research and evidence-informed practice. This means that we now know more than ever before about what is proven to make a difference to pupils' learning.

It is important to note that one of the common findings across all the global research is that:

'Great teaching is the most important lever schools have to improve outcomes for their pupils.' (EEF)

Whilst this is true for all pupils, it is especially important for learners who may have additional needs.

'High-quality teaching, differentiated for individual pupils, is the first step in responding to pupils who have or may have SEN. Additional intervention and support cannot compensate for a lack of good quality teaching.' (Source: Special Educational Needs and Disability Code of Practice (p99), Department for Education, January 2015)"

Re-read the extract again, and straight away, experienced SEND parents will be able to see the fundamental problem with relying on Quality First Teaching as a "catch all" approach for every child.

Firstly, Quality First Teaching is applied by schools – especially primary schools – to help them deliver the National Curriculum.

- Section 4 point 2 of The National Curriculum in England Key Stages 1 and 2 Framework document (Sept 2013) states that schools should "ensure that there are no barriers to every pupil achieving."
  (Source:
  https://assets.publishing.service.gov.uk/media/5a81a9abe5274a2e8 ab55319/PRIMARY_national_curriculum.pdf **)**

- **QFT aims to encourage** "higher expectations through higher levels of support" – and as our extract above states: "Whilst this is true for all pupils, it is especially important for learners who may have additional needs."

But as a parent of SEND kids who have been in the UK school system for 11 years and counting, I have yet to understand exactly what those "higher levels of support" (or indeed "differentiation") look like. **Because in my experience at least, they do not exist.**

It is very hard to cite examples of teachers actively supporting either of my children more <u>because of QFT</u>. And in a huge number of cases, the opposite is more usually true.

The expectation most teachers – and QFT - have is that children will "just keep up" with the pace of teaching, no matter what. Those that don't, or can't, do not necessarily receive additional help from the teacher, nor any investigation into why they may be struggling to keep up. And neither nor do children with identified Special Educational Needs. Here's a perfect, real life example:

- A child, let's call them Evan, has:
  - a formal diagnosis of autism and ADHD
  - Dysgraphia (a neurological disability and Specific Learning Difficulty that seriously impairs a child's ability to process information and to write)
  - and a lawfully enforceable EHCP

- **Yet a teacher told Evan's parents** that because they had been teaching for nearly 20 years, and "knew about dysgraphia", that Evan did <u>not</u> need Assistive Technology such as a laptop in that teacher's lessons

Go figure. Because if that is not a teacher (who is supposedly a practitioner of QFT) putting a direct "barrier" to achievement in the way for a SEND child, I don't know what is.

Additionally, QFT refers to Special Educational Needs - but **it does <u>not</u> mention disability.** Again, there is a quiet assumption that any *disability* a child may have:

- is visible / obvious
- is already identified to the teacher and/or is being met by some means somewhere
- does not come with accompanying Special Educational Needs

In fact, QFT puts <u>no</u> requirement on the teacher to actively identify any kind of additional need at all.

Finally, Quality First Teaching "demands".
It "Expects".
It sets "high challenges".

It demands "100% participation".

Those are pretty triggering words to most adults, never mind to a child.

But the far bigger problems for me are exactly what Quality First Teaching "demands" and "expects" - and what it demands and expects of a child with Special Educational Needs and/or Disabilities. Especially when, as we've already seen, QFT has hardened the demands and expectations teachers have of children, placing the onus firmly onto the child to succeed, no matter what – yet makes no real expectation of the teacher to identify needs or adapt to them. The child is just supposed to cope; their level of stress is irrelevant. And their stress response / behaviour in class is never expected – or allowed - to change.
To reiterate for clarity, as Optimus Education have written, QFT

> '... demands 100% participation from the pupils, and sets high and realistic challenges. It does not 'spoon feed', it is challenging and demanding; it expects pupils to be able to articulate their ideas, understanding and thinking by actively promoting pupil talk.'

What if a child *cannot* actively participate in "pupil talk" or group work?

Who decides what level of challenge is "realistic" for every single child in a class of 30?

What if a child cannot cope with the practice of "cold calling" (when a teacher asks a question of a child in class, even though they did not have their hand up to answer).

What if a child is unable to articulate their ideas or process information at the speed a QFT classroom demands, and simply **cannot participate 100%?**

What if the pace of teaching just moves too fast? What if the pace means moving on from a learning element <u>before</u> some kids have embedded that learning element – and so will struggle when a new "building block" or learning element is placed on top?

What if the <u>demand</u> and <u>expectation</u> Quality First Teaching places on a child, <u>with or without SEND</u> .. is just far too much for a child to cope with?

Finally, **QFT is nothing more than a nice idea**. It is a concept developed by teachers, for teachers, and in applying it, it allows teachers to tell themselves what a good job they are doing.

It sounds to parents like A Very Good Thing for their child to receive.

It makes policy makers feel good, because it's a handy epithet that sounds aspirational, professional and pro-active.

BUT:

- QFT is <u>not</u> an element of the National Curriculum, or Teacher's Standards, or the EYFSF
- And more importantly, **it is neither mandatory <u>nor</u> statutory**

So Quality First Teaching actually has no real standing whatsoever (outside of a teacher's own continuous professional development, perhaps).

- Yet I've had QFT pointed out to me by LA commissioning officers as an identifier of whether a child may or may not have SEND.
- I've heard it touted – both by teachers and LA officers - as a SEND intervention.
- I've even seen it mentioned in EHCPs.

The mention of Quality First Teaching has no place whatsoever in a child's EHCP.

And neither LA officers or teachers should be parroting it, either as an indicator of need, or as a SEND intervention.

QFT should <u>never</u> be elevated above mandatory or statutory requirements such as Teacher's Standards or the law.

Yet, when teachers speak to parents about a struggling child, it very often is.

The name alone has, in my opinion, become one of the single most powerful gaslighting tools deployed against parents, because it sounds so plausible and well-meaning as a concept ... but it actually **means nothing whatsoever** when it comes to identifying and genuinely helping children with SEND.

I firmly believe the pressure and demand Quality First Teaching places on children, is one of the biggest threats to those children's success, happiness and wellbeing in school. I also believe it is one of the biggest drivers of the falling mental health in school-age children.

If a teacher or TA is unable to recognise SEND, and QFT doesn't require them to anyway (or a SEND child's diagnosis and/or Plan are simply being ignored because the teacher "expects" the child to be able to participate) then neither Wave 2 nor Wave 3 of QFT are ever going to help.

Quality First Teaching actually <u>forces</u> children who are not coping in the classroom, to mask. (I'll look at masking more in Part 2.)

For now though, we can clearly see that Quality First Teaching does not make every teacher "a teacher of SEND" at all. **It actually does the opposite**

.

Why This Matters To SEND Families:

- The Education Act 1996, the Equality Act 2010, The Children & Families Act 2014 are all Statutory and Mandatory

  ○ Section 19(1) of the Education Act 1996 states:

    "Each local education authority shall make arrangements for the provision of suitable education ..."

  ○ Section 19(6) of the Education Act 1996 confirms that:

    "Suitable" means to provide "**efficient education, suitable to his age, ability and aptitude and any special educational needs he may have**"

  ○ **The Equality Act 2010** applies to <u>all</u> disabled pupils in <u>every</u> school
    - It requires settings to use Anticipatory Duty / to make Reasonable Adjustments for ALL disabled pupils
    - These requirements are Statutory and non-delegable. That means they are <u>not</u> <u>optional!</u>

  ○ **The Children & Families Act 2014*** contains the statutory rights which ensure children with Special Educational Needs receive the educational provision required as a result of their needs.

    ○ In particular, Section 42 of the Children & Families Act 2014 specifies the "duty to secure special educational provision and health care provision in accordance with EHC Plan"

(* - The Children & Families Act 2014 applies in England. Other parts of the UK may have different legislation in force)

- **The National Curriculum is both Statutory and Mandatory**

- **EYFSF is both Statutory and Mandatory**

- **Teacher's Standards are also both Statutory and Mandatory**

  - Following and applying them is <u>not</u> optional
  - Any teacher who does not, or cannot, live up to the Statutory requirements of Teacher's Standards is breaking their own professional standards, and acting unlawfully

- **Quality First Teaching is neither statutory <u>nor</u> mandatory**

  - It is a theory of teaching
  - It is <u>not</u> a SEND intervention
  - **Yet it is revered by teachers, and LA commissioning officers, as if it over-rides their own statutory duties, and the law**

Additionally:

- The Early Years Foundation Stage and the SEND Code of Practice both specify that early intervention is vital for children who are struggling

- Yet many SEND children reach High School before their needs are even **identified** (never mind diagnosed!)

- Each Key Stage of education assumes the stage before will have caught any Special Educational Needs or disability

- The further up the school system a child goes, the harder it is for the child to have their needs identified, because:

- Command and control "behaviour policies" get stricter, the older a child gets (more on those later)

- The expectations and demands of QFT increase, the older a child gets

- Yet it's assumed any Special Educational Need or disability a child have will be
  - obvious (rather than "invisible", like autism or ADHD)

  - already identified

  - already be being met by someone, somewhere

Quality First Teaching does <u>not</u> meet the needs of the vast majority of children.

Instead, it causes many children to feel pressured, stressed and anxious, because many of them simply <u>cannot</u> keep up. It allows no time and space for children to just "be": to learn in a way that actually suits any individual learning style, nor to absorb, process and actually "do learning" at the pace many of them need to. Children are forced to constantly move on, at pace, **whether essential elements have been taught, learned and properly embedded or not.**

The blame for this pace and rigour is often placed, certainly in English schools, at the door of the Gove reforms made to the National Curriculum in 2014. But no-one ever questions whether any other factors are also playing a role in children's in-school experiences. Factors like:

- the application of Quality First Teaching
- the very rigid "Command and Control" that exists in most schools' "behaviour policies" (and which I'll talk about in more detail in Part 2)

These two aspects of school cause an ever-increasing level of demand and stress to be placed upon children: demand and stress which never lets up, and only increases as the child moves through each Key Stage.

Yet the child is never expected to do anything other than comply. Their behaviour is rigidly controlled by often psychotically strict "behaviour policies" that can see a child given a sanction even just for breathing too loudly, or putting their head on the desk.

No-one in the profession – in my experience at least – stops to ask what effects this might having. As well as blaming the National Curriculum, the media (and sometimes the teaching profession too) also loves to blame OFSTED for many of the problems currently happening in schools. I'll come back to OFSTED again in Part 2, but for now, I'll just say this: **Whether we love it or hate it as an organization, OFSTED did not develop or apply Quality First Teaching: Teachers did.**

The media, and the teaching profession, also love to carp on about the impact of the Covid pandemic on children's "behaviour". But they forget one very important fact: **Behaviour is Communication.** No child who is happy, settled, feeling safe and supported ever "acts up" just for the fun of it. If children are not "behaving", it's because they are unhappy about something in their environment.

The pandemic undoubtedly had a massive and damaging effect on the social and emotional wellbeing of a whole generation of children; it's true impact will not be fully known for years. But let's not deceive ourselves: school-age children in the UK were struggling with unhappiness*, deteriorating mental health, unmet need and a perceived growth in "bad behaviour" long before the pandemic caused this crisis to literally explode into full public view. (I'll come back to the issue of mental health in much more detail in Part 2).

tes

Teaching & Learning - Scotland Leadership - Newsletters Jobs and more -

UK pupils among the world's unhappiest

New Pisa report also finds UK teenagers are more anxious about testing than their counterparts in almost any other country including South Korea and China; and have high internet usage associated with poor test scores.

19th April 2017, 10.01am

Helen Ward

(* - Credit: TES - https://www.tes.com/magazine/archive/uk-pupils-among-worlds-unhappiest

I would hazard a guess that what the media refers to as an "epidemic" of "ghost children" missing from school:

- the huge numbers of families de-registering their children from school to move to Elective Home Education (whether through choice, or because they are being bullied / "intelligence cleansed" out of mainstream schools)

- or parents like me who for whom EHE isn't an option, so have had no choice but to keep our children home from school for extended periods in order to preserve their mental health

has far more to do with the "combat stress" schools put on children, than it has to do with the Covid pandemic anymore.

But I would hazard an even bigger guess that we can actually trace many of the roots of this issue, and the deep and growing unhappiness amongst UK school children, **directly back to 2008 - and the introduction of Quality First Teaching.**

Let's Talk About School Governors

Before we finish looking at how and why UK schools operate the way they do, let's take a look at one last role within education that is absolutely critical to the way our children's schools are run.

Most parents will be aware their child's school has a Board of Governors. And for most parents, that's where their awareness of the Governors begins and ends! But being a school governor is actually a really important role.

People apply to be school governors for a whole variety of reasons:

- they work in a particular field, or have professional knowledge, that they consider relevant to the running of a school
- they really like kids
- they value education
- their child / grandchild is a pupil at the school
- they would like to "give something back" to their community
- they have retired and have a bit of time on their hands
- they are a qualified teacher but no longer work in the classroom setting
- they would like the kudos in the school playground
- it looks good on their CV

Whatever the actual reasons, I am sure the people who step up to be school governors do so with the best of intentions. Their role grew out of those same 19th century roots that much of our UK school system grew from - philanthropists and church leaders saw a desperate need, and just like with the Workhouses before them, small groups of wealthy or influential people began trying to meet that need (for education, for self-improvement, or just for a better standard of worker) by setting up schools.

Governing these new schools wasn't a full time job, but it was a very worthy and worthwhile one.
That image of "the well-meaning School Governor" has never really gone away. Being a school governor is still seen as more of a hobby, something someone does in their spare time, rather than as a meaningful role with any serious operational or legal ramifications. And school governorship remains a voluntary role - the only payment you might receive is to have expenses reimbursed when, for example, you attend a training course.

Parents get to vote on some of the appointments (usually the role of the Parent Governors), but taking part in the vote for governors isn't really seen as being very important by the majority of parents - **and it isn't sold to them as being important either.**

So if any parents do bother to take part in the vote at all, they usually make their choice on the back of a "personal statement", or whether they know the person they are voting for, and not much more.

Yet one of the main driving reasons behind the government policy of Academisation in schools was to drive better educational outcomes for children, better teaching practice, **and better School Governance.**
The idea was that Academies would attract more people from professional backgrounds to be school governors. Those people would then apply their professional knowledge to the Academy. The Academy would benefit, driving up outcomes, and showing the way on "best practice" for other Academies and LA-controlled schools to follow.

I'm not going to go into a deep dive on Academies here; suffice it to say Academies occupy just as many "top of the table" *and* 'bottom of the table" positions as LA-controlled schools do.

(See this article from The Guardian, published in March 2024 for further reading: https://www.theguardian.com/commentisfree/2024/mar/14/the-guardian-view-on-multi-academy-trusts-disputes-over-school-budgets-point-to-deeper-issues Image Credit: The Guardian)

Whether a school is an Academy, or LA-controlled, the governors tend to be voted in by a small number of the total number of families at any given school, usually on the back of not much information, and with not many candidates to choose from.

After a DBS check and some other sort of due diligence (we all assume!), the lucky winner is appointed as a governor, with probably not a great deal more scrutiny of that person's actual knowledge / skillset / aptitude or suitability to act as an effective governor, by anyone outside of the Board of Governors itself: a Board which was also very likely to have been appointed with the same lack of scrutiny of its actual skillset.

Once the election cycle is over, everyone outside the Board pretty much forgets that the school governors even exist.

Here's the problem: Being a school governor is actually a really serious business

The word Governance means:

> "The way that organizations or countries are managed at the highest level, and the systems for doing this" (Source: https://dictionary.cambridge.org/dictionary/english/governance)

The Chartered Governance Institute website says:

> "Governance is a system that provides a framework for managing organisations. It identifies who can make decisions, who has the authority to act on behalf of the organisation and who is accountable for how an organisation and its people behave and perform. Governance enables the management team and the board to run organisations legally, ethically, sustainably, and successfully, for the benefit of stakeholders, including shareholders, staff, clients and customers, and for the good of wider society." (https://www.cgi.org.uk/professional-development/discover-governance/looking-to-start-a-career-in-governance/what-is-governance#:~:text=Governance%20is%20a%20system%20that,its%20people%20behave%20and%20perform.)

So, we can already see that **genuine governance** is pretty high-level stuff, certainly as far as the wider world of business is concerned - exactly the type of person Academies were meant to be attracting as their governors.

So how does that relate to such a vital role in a school, when that role is both **unsalaried** and **voluntary**, and is, to be blunt, appointed on little more than hope?

On the Inspiring Governance website (Inspiring Governance is an organisation run by the Education & Employers charity and funded by the DfE) they describe the role of a school governor as:

- Approving the budget and overseeing the financial performance of the school to make sure money is well spent
- Appointing and holding the headteacher to account for the educational performance of the school and its pupils
- Ensuring clarity of vision, ethos and strategic direction

(Source: https://www.inspiringgovernance.org/volunteers/about-the-role/ 2023)

That's actually a pretty specialist skillset! It's a skillset that's more akin to being a senior Director, rather than an ordinary person who'd like to "do something good" with their time.

Also on the Inspiring Governance website they have a section that's titled:

What's in it for me?

Being part of a governing board will give you experience of working at a strategic level and the opportunity to learn and practice skills that have a direct relevance to employers. These include:

- strategic leadership
- budget control
- data analysis
- staff recruitment
- building relationships and networks
- effective teamworking
- communication
- problem solving
- influencing/negotiation

(Source: https://www.inspiringgovernance.org/volunteers/about-the-role/)

What I find really disturbing about this whole section is

- **Only once** does it mention any need for knowledge of (or interest in) children, or their education

- Any knowledge of, or interest in, special educational needs and/or disabilities **does not get a single mention at all.**

Instead, the "pitch" this site is making veers very strongly towards recruiting governors for Multi-Academy Trusts (not stand-alone LA run schools), and seems to me to treat school governorship as a small-scale version of "The Apprentice".

It is clearly trying to appeal to a younger-than-your average-school-governor demographic, and feels more like an opportunity to take part in a business transaction, rather than to engage with a supremely important role that will determine the life chances of potentially hundreds of young children - **many of whom will have Special Educational Needs and/or Disabilities.**

Why This Matters for SEND Families:

Being a school governor is so much more important than just a business transaction or a nice hobby

- Governors have a massive influence on the culture and direction of a school

- The governors' skill sets when dealing with SEND issues are absolutely critical

  - For example, when a school or setting is named in Section I of a child's EHCP, **the Board of Governors** will be involved with the enquiry from the LA as to whether the setting can meet the child's needs

- **Yet the governors' genuine, lived knowledge of Special Educational Needs and Disabilities is likely to be zip**

- ○ How can someone with the list of skills and qualities on the Inspiring Governance page - and NO knowledge of SEND - make critical decisions for a SEND child?

The role of a school governor has lawful obligations too. If you ever happen to be struggling to sleep, you can read the full regulations here: The School Governance (Roles, Procedures and Allowances) (England) Regulations 2013 (https://www.legislation.gov.uk/uksi/2013/1624/made)

If you manage to wade your way through that document, you'll find school governors do not just hold the lawful responsibility for ensuring a whole raft of requirements and regulations are met: they are also ultimately a Headteacher's boss.

Yet the way school governors are appointed means many just do not have the necessary knowledge of how to hold a school, or a Head, to account - especially when it comes to SEND.

Despite the original aims of Academisation to improve school governance, many school governors still come from an education background themselves - because that's assumed to be "A Really Good Thing" for a school governor to have. It implies educational experience. It implies knowledge that a "lay person" from outside of the profession may not have.

But that means the candidates who come forward are highly likely to be institutionalised into doing and seeing things from a *teacher's* point of view - all the while having no actual experience of governing a school at all.

Many of the candidates who have the time to put themselves forward are just not suited to such a critically important leadership and governance role - and especially not when it's done in a voluntary capacity.

Additionally, and perhaps more worryingly for parents, Part 6(2) of The School Governance Regulations states that governors (with my emphasis):

> 2) In exercising their functions the governing body shall—
>
> (a) act with integrity, objectivity and honesty and <u>in the best interests of the school</u>

We may wish to understand that phrase as meaning "all" of the school, in its entirety – an understanding which would include all stakeholders, including the children who actually learn at the school, and their parents. I think most parents would very much like to read that sentence in that context, and assume they are correct to do so.

However, that is – in my experience at least – **not** the understanding most school governors have of their role at all:

- They see their role as being protective of **The School**, solely as an institution
- They do not – in my experience – really want to "get into the weeds" of how The School interacts with either
  - o the children who attend
  - o or their parents
  in any way that might be even remotely critical of what The School (or the governors themselves) actually do

And that is a massive problem for parents – particularly for SEND parents – when things start to go wrong for their child.

"Bringing in the Governors"

The majority of parents will only ever make contact with their child's school governors when there is a problem that has failed to be dealt with elsewhere within the school's hierarchy. Many of those parents will have children with Special Educational Needs and/or Disabilities.

By the time it comes to a governor's attention, usually but not always via a school's Complaints Procedure (more on those later), the problem parents need help with will have already elevated from the classroom teacher, to the SENCO, to the Head, usually becoming more urgent, more complex, more emotionally-charged, and more desperately needing a resolution, with every increasing step.

The child is, more often than not, already in crisis. Parents hope that by "bringing in the Governors", they will be able to get some accountability, an independent set of ears, someone who will be able to see through the fog and provide guidance and help where everyone else lower down the school has failed.

But as we've already seen, there's a fundamental flaw with

- the way school governors are appointed
- the voluntary nature of their role
- <u>and</u> the view the vast majority of school governors actually take of their role, when it comes to what "the best interests" of the school actually mean

To give you an example, one parent I spoke to recently had contacted their child's school governors asking them to intervene in a very serious matter, where the school was quite clearly failing to fulfil a child's EHCP. First of all, the governor objected to the parent making what they called "serious allegations" - but then did not investigate what those "serious allegations" actually were, or whether they had any basis. The governor then became increasingly defensive, and eventually wrote back to the parent saying they would no longer engage in the conversation.

That is not providing "governance": that is actively choosing to shut down a conversation the governor did not like the sound of.

The governor chose to side with the school, and not support a parent with some very real, and very serious concerns. That parent's experience is not an isolated incident, and I will share a story later that demonstrates exactly why I think it is completely wrong to still call this body of people "Governors".

Because in mine and many other SEND families' experience, **school governors are not actually providing any "governance"** – in the truest, modern business-related sense of the word - <u>at all</u>.

Why This Matters For SEND Families:

- Being a school governor is a *voluntary* role - not a profession

- The governors are the Head's boss

- Many school governors come from an education background

- When a school is failing a SEND child, parents hope the governors will be able to bring clarity, oversight and meaningful help

  BUT!

- Few school governors have the **specific management or communication skills** needed to provide **effective governance**

- The School Governance (Roles, Procedures and Allowances) (England) Regulations 2013 require the governors to act **"in the best interests of the school"** – which may *not* align with the best interests of the children who attend that school (or their families)

- School governors have probably received just as little training in SEND law as the teachers. Many also have little or no lived experience of SEND

- The governors' viewpoint of what SEND means is most likely informed by what the teachers, or the LA, tell them

- Governors will tend to follow the school's lead, and so frame the child, or their parents, as "difficult"

- They will tend to view SEND need as a "behavioural issue" which needs discipline, rather than as a genuine expression of disability/need

- **Failing to meet SEND law in a school is <u>not</u> small stuff!**
  - Being a school governor is a really serious business
  - Such a serious role should not be left to volunteers
  - <u>But it is</u>

- **Every person in a school system is required to meet the expectations placed on them by**
  - The Early Years Framework
  - Teacher's Standards / Teaching Assistant's Standards
  - The School Governance (Roles, Procedures and Allowances) (England) Regulations 2013
  - SEND Law

  - **But they can't. And they don't. And the results for SEND children are devastating**

School Complaints Procedures (And Why, Frankly, Schools Can Shove Them)

School Complaints Procedures are generally put together by senior school leaders, governors and Head Teachers.

We've already explored why that might pose a bit of a problem!

The other problem with School Complaints Procedures is they basically hand all the power to the school - giving parents pretty much no say at all.

Let's remember after all, that The School Governance (Roles, Procedures and Allowances) (England) Regulations 2013 actually require the governors to act **"in the best interests of the school"** – a phrase open to interpretation, and so *not* necessarily in the interests of the children who attend that school, or their families.

That automatic bias towards the "best interests of the school" means School Complaints policies and procedures are not fit for purpose, or providing support to families, and/or bringing accountability to schools when things have gone wrong.

School complaints procedures are not just very authoritarian (for which we can read "pro-school / anti-parent"), they are also usually designed for the "small stuff" of school life - the stuff the people who write School Complaints Procedures *expect* parents to complain about:

"Mohammed isn't allowed indoors at break time"
"Leah pushes my kid in the dinner queue"
"Jaime's bag keeps getting kicked around the cloakroom"
"Ravi gets too much homework for a 4 year old"
"Connor didn't get picked for the school play"
"Aisha keeps writing on my kid's jumper"
"Sammy's coat has gone missing"

"Small stuff" is what schools *wish* parents only ever complained about, because it's very, very easy to deal with. But as we've already seen:

- Failing to see a child's so-called "bad behaviour" for what it really is - i.e. communicating unmet SEND need - is not "small stuff"

- Creating trauma for a SEND child because their school environment is failing to meet their needs, is not "small stuff"

- **Failing to comply with THE LAW is not "small stuff"**

These things are the very definition of Big Stuff.

And School Complaints policies and procedures are absolutely not set up to deal with Big Stuff in a way that is fit for purpose.

But because schools speak a different language to SEND parents, schools (especially Primary schools) tend to treat every complaint as if it is "small stuff": a little issue that can be happily tidied away with a quick chat (i.e. gaslighting – more on that later) after school, to get the parent to see things the teacher's way.

When that fails, the teacher, or you, might bring in the SENCO to join the - increasingly unfriendly - "friendly chat".
The next level after that is to bring in the Head.
If we are *really* going for it, you might get to finally meet one of the governors (or at least get an email from them.)

And at some stage, someone will point you to the School Complaints Procedure, and tell you (quite firmly - because now you are being a Naughty Parent and not playing the game the school's way) that their Complaints Procedure is the only way you are allowed to have your complaint dealt with.

Spoiler Alert : IT DOESN'T WORK

I have spent far too much of my life reading and digesting far too many school policies:

- Behaviour Policies
- Attendance Policies
- SEND Policies
- Inclusion Policies
- Complaints Procedures

In my experience, the majority of LA-controlled Primary school policies read more like a Wish List than an actual Policy with Key Performance Indicators, or meaningful governance, or measurable outcomes, or a genuine means to resolve very real problems.

Academy Trust and/or High School policies tend to be rather more formal, and whilst they may have a bit more meat to them as far as content goes, they are also very deliberately written to make it very clear to parents who is in charge of the complaints process (Clue: it's not you). For example, one of the schools my kids have been through declared in their Complaints Policy that if a parent is not satisfied with the outcome of any investigation the school does into their complaint, that they (the parents):

- **have no right of appeal**
- and that if they then continue to complain about the same issue, **their actions will be considered "vexatious"** and may result in the school taking legal action against the parents

Whatever stance a school takes, from the most woolly and ill-defined to the most formally-written and aggressive policies, and even the ones that quote the under-pinning law, these Policies are usually written by people, and/or school governors, who do not understand:

- what SEND families' experiences of the school system are really like
- what SEND children's needs truly are

- why parents are fighting so hard to have their children's needs met
- or how SEND law truly applies to SEND kids and their needs in an educational setting

Or if we are being *really* cynical, these policies are written by people who absolutely <u>do</u> understand SEND law/how it applies to SEND children in school, and who fully understand its potential impact on how a school or Academy Trust operates .. **but who don't want to create the bother of actually applying SEND law, y'know, lawfully.**

That would be a lot of hard work.

It would probably be quite expensive.

It would involve a very different culture to the one the majority of schools / Academies operate on.

Far better to use some legal terms and references, and/or some veiled threats, to make our Policy look quite big and scary, and to make any puny parent think long and hard before even going there, right?

Why This Matters for SEND Families

- Schools and governors speak the language of attendance, attainment, behaviour and discipline

    o So school Complaints Procedures are written from that point of view

- Parents speak the language of care, emotion, needs and the damage being done to a child by negative experiences in the school environment

    o School Complaints Procedures have no room for any of those things

- In spite of a lot of recent media reports, most parents (and *especially* SEND parents) do not complain to schools "vexatiously" / just because they feel like it
    - Parents, and especially SEND parents, complain to schools when things are going really badly wrong
    - When SEND parents needs to complain, their complaint and their child's needs more often than not have law attached to them
    - By the time a complaint is lodged against a school, a child's wellbeing and/or mental health is usually at stake
    - School complaints procedures make no allowance for that whatsoever: they focus far more on proving the school is "right" (and, by default, that the parents/child are "wrong")

- **The Law over-rides any and every school policy - particularly if that policy is not compliant with the Law:**
    - The Children & Families Act 2014
    - The Equality Act 2010
    - The Education Act 1996
    and so on, all apply

- Many school policies are written to look and sound like they are compliant with the Law

    - but even if the wording is compliant with the Law, the way those policies are interpreted or enacted by teachers, heads and governors, **is very often not compliant with the Law**

    - Yet most families do not have the knowledge, or the means, to hold anyone to account for unlawful failings – **and schools and LAs know it**

To close Part 1:

Let's see how some of these professional standards, expectations and "the social contract" have played out in real life, for a real life SEND child.

Let Me Tell You A Story ...

I always took Big Bruv to toddler groups and activities, right from being a very tiny baby. Big Bruv and I always had a lovely time singing the songs, playing some games .. He didn't usually join in with other children and only really wanted to play with me - but that was ok. He was only a toddler after all.

As he got a bit older, and by the time I was pregnant with Little Sis, he would get very upset every time I left the room. Another mum, a very dear friend, kindly suggested that maybe he would benefit from going to a creche a couple of times a week, "You know, to help him get used to you not being there all the time - especially with the new baby on the way. It really helped my eldest when they were struggling. And it's good prep for school."

So, I would drop Big Bruv off at our local creche - just for a couple of hours, to help him socialise, to help him "get ready" for school nursery, and to help him "get used" to being cared for by people other than me for short spaces of time.

Sometimes, he just couldn't manage it.
He would cry like his little heart was breaking.
"It's separation anxiety," the staff told me. "It's perfectly normal. Most children struggle with being left at first. Just leave him with us, mum. He's always fine after you go, he'll soon get used to it."

But he didn't get used to it.

So instead of "getting a break", or getting a few jobs done to prepare for a new baby arriving, I would spend those couple of hours on tenter hooks in the cafe next door to the creche. Because the staff and I knew perfectly well that, more often than not, I would get a friendly tap on the window from one of the creche workers, asking me to pop in and be with Big Bruv to help him settle.

And when I was there, he could settle.

When I wasn't, he struggled more often than he didn't.

"He'll be fine," the staff would say. "All completely normal. He'll soon grow out of it."

When Big Bruv turned 3, just like every other parent we knew through creche and local toddler groups, we enrolled him into the local school nursery. It was a very big, and very busy nursery - so big, it had 2 classrooms, and 2 rotations of around 40 children each day: one in the morning and one in the afternoon.

Big Bruv started attending in the afternoon group.

He would "act up" all the way there – either crying, "tantrumming", refusing to walk (but also refusing the buggy or a trike), or finding the single most interesting crack in the pavement to stare at for as long as possible ...

Or if he wasn't "acting up" .. well, he just looked so obviously sad to be going.

He hated his key worker, to the point that he wouldn't even speak to her.

He would often stay in the cloakroom and refuse to leave my side – especially if his key worker was nearby.

"It's perfectly normal," the staff would say to me. "He's always fine after you go, just leave him with us!"

And someone would take his little hand from mine, and lead him into the nursery.

It didn't take long for Big Bruv, at the tender age of 3, to start locking himself in our bathroom on nursery days, to show me just how much he really <u>didn't</u> want to go.

Long Road Dad and I went into the nursery to have a chat with the staff about what might be happening for Big Bruv.

"There's nothing wrong," they said. "He's absolutely fine when he's here."

What we didn't realise at that time, was we were having, not our first but our second experience of "We Are Not Seeing It."

Our first had actually happened at the creche. We just hadn't known.

Once again, in a different setting, we were being absolutely assured that Big Bruv was "100% fine" whenever we left him, and that we just needed to let him "get used to it".

The nursery was attached to the local primary school, and after not really getting anywhere with the lead at the nursery, the School Head invited us to a meeting and told us very clearly:

"Big Bruv is absolutely fine when he's here. I have observed him in the nursery. I am the professional, my staff are all professionals, and we are telling you: There is nothing wrong."

This led to our first experience of "The Home To School" book. We were also having our first unspoken experience of "It Must Be A Home Problem".

For the record, the "Home to School" book is a total misnomer.

It is meant to be there for school (or in this case the nursery), to tell you all the great things that have happened for your child whilst they were in the setting, and how very, very happy your child is there.

It's a device to tell you "Your child is fine _whenever they are with us_.." (in other words, raised eyebrow, question mark, what do you make of that mum and dad..?)

We quickly learned that, as Big Bruv's parents, we were meant to read and absorb everything in that book, and take it as gospel.

And we were also meant to absorb the message that our child really was "fine" .. _when we were not there._

But we were absolutely <u>not</u> meant to write anything in that book ourselves - especially <u>not</u> about how increasingly hard our child was finding it to even set foot in their nursery in the first place. Oh no, none of that "negative" input was welcome at all, thank you very much! This was strictly a one-way communication! We must focus on the positives!

It didn't matter if Big Bruv had slow-timed, or just cried his eyes out, the whole way there. Or that he'd run upstairs and taken all his clothes off just as we were about to leave the house, so he might not have to go ...

What mattered was this was a one-way communication to tell us, the parents, that we were <u>wrong</u>.

And that our child was actually "<u>fine</u>".

In the end, we decided we couldn't ignore our son's difficulties any longer. He was struggling terribly. We didn't know why. And no-one was able to give us any insight or answers or ideas, except to keep doing more of the same until he "got used to it".

But surely we could all see that approach wasn't working .. couldn't we?

Long Road Dad and I could.

But it was as if we were speaking a totally different language to the nursery, and they just couldn't understand what we were trying to say. i.e. surely this isn't (for want of a better word) "normal"? Surely all kids don't find nursery so hard?

Whatever the case, we now knew we didn't want our child to stay there any longer, or for him to go to that attached primary school, with that Head. And we would not want to put our daughter there either. The staff clearly didn't "get" our son at all. And if they couldn't get him, they might not get our daughter if she started having the same difficulties at the same age.

After doing a lot of research, we chose for Big Bruv a small, village primary school with less than a hundred pupils. The setting was idyllic, with beautiful views of the countryside and a gorgeous, well-tended garden outside the Reception classroom for the children to grow stuff and enjoy messy play in.

The Head assured us they had listened to us, and that they had understood all the difficulties Big Bruv had had at nursery.

They promised us most sincerely they would take very good care of our son.

They promised us that quality first teaching would fill any gaps, and that our son would thrive under their care.

With less than 30 children in his entire year group, we felt certain there was no way Big Bruv could "fall through the cracks" like he seemed to have done at that big, busy nursery!

The staff would be able to see him, really get to know him, help him, support him. He would feel more secure in a small, tightly knit village school with 100 or so children, than in a big city "super school" with over 500 children.

This was going to be exactly the right choice for him.

And for a couple of years, it was just that.

"He does drift off quite a bit!" his classroom teachers would tell us. "And he's very forgetful!" But other than that, the play-based curriculum of Reception, Year 1 and Year 2 really seemed to suit him. He was hitting his milestones. He read well. He could write. He had a lovely little group of friends. He seemed really settled.

Then Key Stage 2 happened...

Suddenly, it wasn't ok to play, or wander around the classroom or chat to your friends: the expectation was to spend far more time sitting in your seat, staying very very still, listening to the teacher, and doing a lot more writing.

Year 3 was a bit of a mixed bag - not exactly thriving, not exactly falling behind either. But Big Bruv wasn't really enjoying things very much.

In Year 4, Big Bruv's classroom teacher was also the school SENCO. At this point we didn't even know what a SENCO was! But what we did know was that this teacher had a great reputation with all the parents in the school, and that we felt we could trust them.

Strangely though, that teacher/SENCO was giving us a very mixed message about our son.

On the one hand, we were being told "He is fine in school."

That he was happy.

That he was settled.

That he was hitting all his attainment milestones.

And on the other, we were being given a sub-text of "He is actually quite an annoying child to teach, because he's never "ready to learn", he never sits still, doesn't really do as we ask, and he never pays any attention."

Big Bruv was also having quite a few problems in his relationship with the class TA - and that meant he was finding it harder to get into school each day. The refusals, the slow timing, the crying in the car, the refusal to go inside when the bell rang - they all told us something was going wrong (again).

The teacher/SENCO suggested maybe a "Home To School" book would be a good idea?

At that point, we knew we were in trouble.

Because once again, the "Home To School" book was most definitely a one-way conversation - and it was mostly telling us how crap our kid was.

Big Bruv was struggling to sit in his seat for long periods.

He would make random shout-outs.

He would decline to get his books and pencils out of his tray.

He was never "ready to learn".

He would get up and start wandering around the classroom, asking other children what they were doing.

He fidgeted non-stop.

He was inattentive.

He was disruptive and unco-operative.

His handwriting was deemed to be appalling and not up to the expected standard.

The very strong implication was that he was actually quite lazy.

The other very strong implication was that we (as mum and dad) needed to "sort out" his behaviour, and make sure he knew this sort of thing just wasn't acceptable in school.

He, and we, needed to understand these types of behaviours were not only not meeting the school's expectations of our child, but the school considered them to be no longer age appropriate.

We had to work harder at making him become more independent.

We had to teach him resilience.

We had to stop mollycoddling him by doing things like packing his swimming bag or PE bag for him (even though there was no way in hell he could manage that by himself .. so to save him the shame of having to borrow stuff from lost property, we would pack his bag for him).

The underlying message was if Big Bruv couldn't do these things by himself yet, then he jolly well needed to learn to do it by himself! Because he was growing up now and this sort of thing was no longer acceptable!

"It's not us," was the underlying message coming through loud and clear from almost everyone, from the TA who took him to swimming each week, right up to the Head.

"Be better parents," they seemed to be saying. "Because this must be a home problem: he is absolutely fine in school!"

And yet .. we knew in our hearts that he wasn't.

At this point the teacher/SENCO suggested maybe our child needed to be discussed by the local panel of Educational Psychologists.

We had no idea what that meant or what the implications might be - but the way the request was put to us felt less like an offer of help and support, and far more like a veiled threat.

No-one took the time to explain to us how an Ed Psych intervention might actually help our son. Instead, the implication was "There is something psychologically wrong with your child or he wouldn't be acting this way. His behaviour is unacceptable. This is your fault. You are bad parents. Sign here and let us bring in the psychs."
Naturally, the very idea scared the hell out of us.
We politely but firmly declined. And that was the end of that - no other support was offered.

By year 5, Big Bruv's difficulties were impossible to ignore. He had a wonderful classroom teacher that year, one all the kids in the school adored. But even that teacher was not able to get a real handle on his needs - partly because they didn't have any strategies or approaches in their toolbox that worked for Big Bruv for anything more than a few days at a time.
To add to the problem, everything good his teacher did to support him was being promptly undone by the same overzealous TA whom Big Bruv had had in Year 4 (and whom by now he absolutely hated), every time his kind, funny, nurturing teacher was out of the room.

It's not unfair to say this particular TA seemed to have had quite enough of "all this nonsense" from Big Bruv, and had made it their personal mission to shame and/or punish whatever this "behaviour" was out of him at every given opportunity ... All of which just drove his distress and hatred of school, and his deep sense of panic whenever his best-beloved teacher was out of the classroom, even deeper.
We knew his distress and panic were there: he told us about them (even though he was only young, he was incredibly articulate).
He also showed them in his behaviours every morning before school.
He showed them in his anger and frustration when he got home every afternoon.

He showed them with his growing anxiety and his rapidly disintegrating meltdowns, every time a weekend, or a school holiday, was coming to an end.

But still the overarching message from the Head, and by now the Governors was "He is fine in school".

The school even took the trouble of springing a Very Senior Person from the Academy Trust into a meeting (without letting me in on the surprise first!), to tell me in no uncertain terms:
"Everything is fine. The Head has told you everything is fine. So it's not the school. It's your kid. It's you."

Yet no matter how many times they said it to us, from an increasingly senior line of people, the truth was plainly clear: **Big Bruv was absolutely <u>not</u> "fine" in school. And both we, and he, knew it.**

By this time we had been telling the school for some months that we believed Big Bruv was autistic and that he needed an urgent assessment.
"No no, it's all perfectly normal," the Head would say to me. "He's not autistic. We are the professionals. We would know. He's always fine after you go, just leave him with us."
Then they, or a different TA to the one he hated, or his teacher, would take his hand from mine, and lead him into the school.
The silent panic on Big Bruv's face as I left him, haunted me.
Many days, I walked back across the playground with tears rolling down my face.

That was on the days when he actually got out of the car: there were plenty of others when he simply couldn't get out of the car. We'd had to stop walking even any short distance to school and drive to the school gates instead, because even seeing the school building up the road caused him so much distress.

Eventually the morning meltdowns were so big and explosive, and his distress was so great, that if we had even made it as far as the school, there was no option but to turn the car around and take him home for his own safety.

Then one day, in *yet another* meeting (this time with the Very Important Person from the Academy Trust *and* the Chair of Governors no less) we were directly told that we were to blame for our child's problems **because we had turned down the offer of Educational Psychology over a year ago.**

We were told that a referral for an autism assessment had been made – but no-one could evidence when, or by whom, or tell us what the process or timeline for assessment was.
We were then told we were "overcommunicating".
That we were being "unacceptably hostile".
And that we were "demanding too much" of the school.
But at the same time, we were also being told our child was "fine".

Then something momentous happened: Big Bruv had *the mother of all meltdowns,* right outside the room we were all sitting in.

We could all hear him: our spirited, characterful, but also emotionally very private child, who really *desperately* did not want to stand out, and who could only show his true feelings, his true anguish about school to us .. was literally screaming in distress at the Head.
It was an absolute loss of control, where he simply could not hold his feelings in any longer.
And it was taking place in the most public part of the building, where everyone in that tiny village school could see him, hear him, and witness his complete mental and emotional collapse, right there as it happened.

A silent look went around the meeting room. The game was up.
We took Big Bruv and Little Sis home. They never went back to that school.

The End. (or so we thought...)

Why This Mattered So Much To Our Family:

Big Bruv's school environment should never have been so hostile to him and his needs, that it drove him to a trauma-induced emotional breakdown.

He was just a young child - yet he had spent his entire school career struggling, pretending not to feel how he really felt in school so he didn't "look different", masking his difficulties with writing, with processing, with sensory overload, with being undiagnosed autistic and undiagnosed ADHD .. and now his coping mechanism wasn't working any more.

The only way left for him to express his distress was the absolute and very public collapse of a total meltdown in school.

- Big Bruv's needs <u>should</u> have been picked up by trained professionals applying the Early Years Foundation Stage framework.

- If the EYFS didn't catch him, his needs <u>should</u> have been picked up by trained teachers applying the requirements of the National Curriculum − or at the very least, the stepped approach of their own system: Quality First Teaching.

- A TA <u>should</u> have been sufficiently trained to pick up on his difficulties with sensory stimuli, attention and handwriting - *even if he was masking*

- A school's position "in loco parentis" should have triggered a duty of care once his parents had reported his difficulties into the school. **But they did not.**

There is also very specific SEND law attached to Big Bruv's needs that his teachers, the SENCO and the school governors, *should* have known about and which *should* have protected him.

But it did not.

Instead, everything that was happening to Big Bruv began to be framed as "School Refusal" – a really insidious term that I'll come back to shortly and that is thankfully now falling out of use. A term which **places blame firmly on the child and the family**, yet does nothing whatsoever to ask WHY the child is struggling so much to come into school.

Why This Matters To SEND Families:

- We can clearly see from Big Bruv's story that the National Curriculum, Teacher's Standards, the Early Years Foundation Stage Framework, even Quality First Teaching, plus a basic duty of care, **and the Law,** did not help Big Bruv at all. (Those same supposed safeguards have not helped Little Sis throughout her school life either).

- Too many children - whether they have SEND or not - fail to receive teaching that genuinely **meets their needs, rather than the teaching profession's "demands" and "expectations".**

- Without the right support and recognition of need early enough in a child's school career

    - many children who "don't look autistic" or just seem to "zone out a bit", and who mask, might never get an intervention, **no matter how much they need it**. Because the teacher, TA or SENCO looks only at the mask - and "does not see"

- any need to escalate a child to greater levels of support
- <u>or</u> that a medical opinion might be needed (we'll look at that more in Part 2)

- When everything else had failed, and we asked the governors for help, they did not have the skills, nor the knowledge and understanding our family needed.
  - They could not, and did not, help
  - Instead, they backed the school against us and our child
  - They did not understand that governors should, in theory, provide "governance"
  - They did not understand SEND law

- And the only offer of help to our family (in the form of a referral to the EdPsych panel) was never explained to us as a positive: instead it was presented like a judgement on our parenting, or (worse still) as a threat

- Everything that happened to Big Bruv was framed as a "refusal" on his part – thereby apportioning blame to us as his parents for not dealing with his "refusal" to attend

  - Yet no-one in the school environment ever asked themselves what the reason for his "refusal" might be
  - Instead, his distress was framed as a "behavioural problem", or a "choice" on his part

- All trust between the school and us was gone; there was no choice left but to leave. This caused massive emotional trauma to our already struggling child:

  - Big Bruv lost all the friends and familiar faces/spaces he had known since the age of 4

○   He had to endure a new trauma:

- starting at a new school
- in a new and much bigger building
- with
  - new routines and systems that he didn't understand
  - new teachers and staff who did not know him or his needs
  - new children who did not know him or his needs

Big Bruv <u>still</u> had no interventions, no support, no diagnosis, not even so much as a My Support Plan … and no recognition whatsoever that he had Special Educational Needs & Disabilities.

Our family had been "intelligence cleansed" out of a school – forced to take our SEND child elsewhere, because his school were "Not Seeing It".

All we had left was the hope that a different school would do things better.

We hoped that changing schools would the end of the story. But it wasn't.

Our story is not unique.   Even within the tiny village school where my children started their journey, many other children struggled, and other families were left with no choice but to leave.

And the same thing is still happening, day in and day out, in mainstream schools all over the country, to families just like mine and yours.

How it started...

How it's going...

© The Long Road

Let Me Tell You <u>Another</u> Story ...

Once upon a time, Big Bruv (and Little Sis) were both intelligence-cleansed out of a small village primary school that "did not see" their difficulties for what they were: undiagnosed Special Educational Needs & Disabilities.

So for Year 4 and Year 6 respectively, Little Sis and Big Bruv moved to a new primary school.

After 7 months, every child in the UK was kicked out of school and into the first Covid lockdown.

Then, having been out of school since the Spring, with no school in between and no transition work having been done, Big Bruv went to High School.

And LongRoadMum and LongRoadDad went on a whole new journey.

Before he went into Year 7, we tried our very best to open the lines of communication with the school, explain to the SENCO what Big Bruv's needs were/just how much he struggled in school, and that he was going to need a lot of transition support.

But because we had no "evidence", we just couldn't get through to them; every concern we had, every need we tried to describe, was batted away by everyone from the SENCO down. They. Did. Not. See. It.

Big Bruv soon began becoming increasingly distressed by school, and increasingly dysregulated at home. We were getting literally nowhere with the SENCO, who was becoming increasingly difficult to get hold of.
Then one day, we ended up in a meeting with a really rather unpleasant individual known as the "Head of Inclusion".

The "Head of Inclusion" was – to put it bluntly – about as open to the idea of genuine inclusion or invisible disabilities, as an electric fence. It was a very horrible, openly hostile meeting, with a horrible and openly hostile individual, who's attitude would probably have been more suited to a military boot camp than a school.

This person gave us, and our newly-engaged SEND Advocate, half an hour of their (obviously very precious) time, and not a second more.
They even deliberately held the meeting in the classroom they would be teaching in, in half an hour's time, just to make sure we really got the message.
They then spent that half hour talking, never listening, and attempting to bully us into being good little parents/quietening down about all this "needs not being met" stuff.
Because our son's needs <u>did not really exist.</u>
They couldn't exist.
Big Bruv did not have A Diagnosis for a start.
He was attending school.
He wasn't throwing chairs around the place or spending his life in the isolation pod - he'd only ever had 1 poxy Demerit, for goodness sake.
And he was hitting all <u>their</u> "attainment markers".

In other words, "We Are Not Seeing It".

It was obvious to us and our Advocate that the school had set their "attack dog" on us; this person basically held our son's future at that school in their hands, and they clearly didn't accept *any* of what we were telling them was happening.
Yet, shortly before our meeting, our son had been so distressed at the prospect of attending school, he had attempted to jump out of the car at 40 mph.
"Don't care," was the jist of the Head of Inclusion's response.
"You're making mine and my team's lives very difficult. Go away."

We decided to escalate our complaint.

We looked up the school's Formal Complaints Procedure.
We followed it to the letter.
And at every stage, whether after a long and carefully put together chain of correspondence, or perhaps a face to face meeting if we were "really lucky", we were stopped in our tracks, told quite emphatically by a rising chain of command that our complaint had been dealt with satisfactorily (whether we thought it had or not was utterly irrelevant!), and that the matter was "settled".

This wasn't new: we'd experienced exactly the same in Big Bruv's nursery, and now also in two different Primary schools.

And yet, Big Bruv now had a diagnosis! A double one, no less, of Autistic Spectrum Condition (I hate the word "disorder") and of ADHD.

We knew we had no choice but to elevate our complaint higher, just to try to be heard.

We took our complaint to the Chair of Governors, and to the Head of the Academy Trust.

That process culminated in a formal and Very Serious Meeting, which was attended by:

- LongRoadMum and LongRoadDad
- Our highly experienced and professional SEND Advocate (whom we had hired in at a cost of several hundred pounds, and who had now been working with us for several months to help us put our son's lawful and needs-based case across to the school)
- The School Head (who was also a Senior Partner on the Board of the Academy Trust. Go figure.)
- A School Governor (not even the Governor responsible for SEND. Again, go figure)

- The Chair of Governors
- An independent Governor from another school, to act as a witness (funnily enough, they were from the Primary School Big Bruv had come from, and which Little Sis currently attended. Once more, go figure.)
- And an independent Meeting Clerk (who was "independent" in the sense that they were appointed by the Academy Trust) to create the official Minutes

LongRoadDad and I fought tooth and nail to be able to take an audio recording of that meeting.
We knew it was a critical one.
And we had already been in far too many of this type of meeting, to know that Minutes taken by schools:

> • are usually heavily biassed against parents and towards the school, and so are unreliable at best
> • invariably miss out all the Really Important Law Stuff. Because the Minuter, often another teacher or a school administrator, generally does not understand just how Really Important that Law Stuff actually is.
> (Or perhaps more cynically, the Minuter <u>does</u> know just how Really Important that Law Stuff is, so chooses to omit it? I'll let you decide.)
> • often mysteriously fail to appear until weeks after the meeting
> By that time, a School Complaints Procedure often also decrees that a Complaint - no matter how serious it may be - has "lapsed", because parents were unable to act fast enough to satisfy the Policy

With all of that in mind, we insisted on making our own recording of that meeting. And the Academy Trust, along with the Chair of Governors, said:

"No. Making your own, personal recording goes against <u>our</u> Security and Data Protection Policies. If you try to take a recording, either openly or secretly, we will stop the meeting and your Complaint will be dismissed outright."

(As a side note, the "data protection" argument is quite a flimsy one and possibly would not stand up to a legal challenge, because this is a meeting full of adults who have chosen to attend, are all able to give informed consent, and who are there solely to talk to you about your child, with your permission ... but I'll leave that one for now)

Not knowing any better at that time, we conceded.
Our fear was that if we didn't back down on that one point, the meeting would not go ahead, and our complaint would be considered to be "Resolved".
We would have nowhere left to go for our son.

We did not want him to have to go through the trauma of changing schools again - he had already been through that before. So we pressed ahead with putting together the most solid case we could, to give this our very best shot.

I spent literally hours going through the Academy Trust's Special Educational Needs policy, and its separate Disability & Inclusion, and Mental Health Policies, and writing up my presentation. I worked on this until way past midnight over several evenings - I had no choice: I was trying to fit this exercise in around my paid day job, and the small matter of being a parent to two SEND kids (one of whom was now in a full-blown school-related mental health crisis ...).

I forensically picked out every individual element of the school's Policies, explaining precisely where and how the school had failed to meet their own policies.
We quoted how the Law actually over-rides all of their in-school policies anyway.
And how the Law (in particular the Children and Families Act 2014, and the Equality Act 2010) all applied in our son's case.

When the meeting finally happened our Advocate, LongRoadDad and I very calmly and methodically presented our points for over an hour and a half, to an increasingly ashen-faced panel.

The independent Governor from another school (the one from Little Sis's school) nodded along, clearly seeing all our points.

The Chair of Governors and their side-kick were more bullish and combative, not wanting to accept all our points (even the unarguable ones about the Law); our Advocate, LongRoadDad and I calmly and methodically ground down their objections with facts and evidence.

By the end of the meeting, the Head Teacher was visibly shaking and looked to be on the verge of tears. The Head apologised to us for the way the school had failed our son. They promised they would learn from this experience, and that they would make sure things were put right for our child. Our son's needs <u>would</u> be met.

We, and the Head, then left the room, and the Panel retired to consider the evidence they had just heard, promising they would report back within a few days.

Long Road Dad and I left that 3 hour meeting at 9pm.
It was dark.
We had had nothing to eat or drink that evening, as we had both come pretty much straight from work.
We were utterly exhausted and emotionally shattered.
But we also left that meeting feeling calmly satisfied that we had stood our ground, and put together a compelling and lawful case. For the first time since our son had begun to struggle at that school (or indeed any of his settings since the age of 4), we had **hope.**
We'd gone higher and further with this complaint than any other we had taken on; we had done so to a thoroughly professional standard, and in microscopic detail. And we had explained <u>exactly</u> how the Law applied to our son, now he had a diagnosis.

Our very experienced SEND Advocate shook our hands as we all parted, and said "You won in there. Well done."

We then went home to relieve the babysitter, and to try to get our two highly anxious kids (who had been utterly freaking out about being left with a babysitter in the first place) to bed.
It was way past both their bedtimes. Big Bruv was on the edge of a meltdown. He could not stop pacing the room, ticcing and stimming all the time, until we gave him a full de-brief of how the meeting had gone.
His anxious outbursts were keeping Little Sis awake; she was completely burnt out with anxiety herself, so was wired as hell too.
It took at least another hour to settle them both.
At about midnight, Long Road Dad and I finally sat down and stared at the wall for a bit. We had a little cry. We had a glass of wine to calm ourselves. Then we went to bed, because we both had work and school runs in the morning.

*****

When the Meeting Minutes, and the decision of the Panel, were finally issued by the "independent Clerk" about 10 days later, our complaint was dismissed in full.

Over 5 pages, their response was the written equivalent of "fingers in ears, la la la, can't hear you."

Or perhaps more to the point: "We Are Not Seeing It".

The Head's apology, given to our faces as they had struggled to hold back tears, had not even gone on the official record - their official record.
That apology, that had been so hard won, that had meant so very much to us, and potentially meant so very much for our son, had been wiped from history. It now only existed in ours and our Advocate's collective memories.

The Minutes also told us that the Panel's decision was final.

That we had no right of Appeal.

Additionally, we were told if we continued any further with any of our complaints, that would be considered "vexatious", and we would be open to legal action from the Academy Trust.

We couldn't see that we had any other options left. At that point, we had no idea that an Education Solicitor might have been able to help, and we didn't have the funds to take that route anyway.

We had no choice but to look for another High School for our son, and put him through the trauma of changing schools.
Again.

He had his diagnosis, but it had changed nothing in the eyes of the school. And he still had no meaningful support plan.

We had no choice left but to hope – once more - that the next school would be better.

The End. (Or so we hoped ... Again.)

Why This Mattered So Much To Our Family – And Why it Matters To Yours:

Once more, Big Bruv's school environment had been so hostile to him and his needs, his distress was so extreme, that it drove him this time to actually try to harm himself by jumping out of a moving car.
This level of distress and mental-health trauma amongst school-age children is very common. (I'll come back to this point again later in Part Two.)

Big Bruv was nearly 12 years old; he had spent the entire **8 years** of his school career to date, struggling, pretending not to feel how he really felt, masking his difficulties with sensory overload and debilitating anxiety. He had hit high school before finally being diagnosed AuDHD (a shorthand term many SEND families now use to describe the double diagnosis of Autism and ADHD).
This scenario is pretty much the standard for SEND kids.

He had also been through the trauma of having to change primary schools months before the start of a global pandemic (due to unmet need), followed by the transition to high school during a pandemic – all with no support whatsoever.

A whole generation of kids went through the Covid pandemic having been pretty much thrown out of school/learning, **with no planning or consideration about how they would be supported in the years afterwards** – just some vague mumblings about "catch up learning". And many of those kids had already been struggling with unmet SEND.

I'm going to reiterate some points here for absolute clarity:

- Big Bruv's needs should have been picked up by trained teachers applying the requirements of the National Curriculum – or at the very least, the stepped approach of their own system: Quality First Teaching. **It did not happen.**

- The statutory Teachers Standards – particularly Teachers Standards #5 - should have been applied, and teachers should have picked up on his needs. **But they did not.**

- A school's position "in loco parentis" should have triggered a basic duty of care, once his parents had reported his difficulties into the school. **But once again, it did not.**

- The very specific law attached to Big Bruv's **now diagnosed** Special Educational Needs and Disability that his teachers, the SENCO, the Head of Inclusion, and the school governors, <u>should</u> have known about and understood, once again <u>should</u> have protected him. **But they did not.**

- With a now-extensive history of extreme anxiety and EBSA on record, along with an actual diagnosis of AuDHD, the SENCO <u>should</u> have done the one job they are supposed to do:

  o They should have investigated his needs further
  o They should have made a referral for more support
  o At the very least they should have understood about masking, and looked beyond the obvious try to work out what going on for our son
  o **But they did not**
  o They were "Not Seeing It"
  o And the assumption was, if any of what we (the parents) were telling the school about our son's distress was actually "real", someone would have done something about/put a support plan in place, much earlier than high school.

- <u>Every</u> system in the school that should – in theory – have protected our son and his mental health, and which should have identified, then supported, his Special Educational Needs and Disabilities .. **had once again failed to do so.**

- And to add insult to injury, **even with a diagnosis**, the very highest level of the school's Complaints Procedure had been literally weaponised against him, and against us as his parents.

Yet again, a school's senior leadership team and its governors had closed ranks on us, placed the blame firmly on our family, and had done nothing whatsoever to ask WHY Big Bruv was struggling SO MUCH ... **or why we, his parents, were fighting so damned hard to be heard.**

Big Bruv now had formal diagnosis, **but no-one actually cared.** In their "expert" opinion, even if he was autistic, even if he had ADHD, and even if his mental health was crashing to the point of trying to hurt himself, his needs were "not big enough" for him to need an EHCP.

We had no choice but to try to find yet another school for our son ... and to hope once again that next time it would be better for him

Big Bruv had been "intelligence cleansed" out of a mainstream school.

AGAIN.

As I said before, our family's story is NOT unique: not by any stretch of the imagination.

And that matters to <u>every</u> SEND family, whether you even know you are a SEND parent yet, or not.

When we actually pull the problem apart and look at its roots, we can clearly see the "social contract" with school/mainstream education is simply not working for huge numbers of children and families.   Because THE SYSTEM is built and designed specifically

- <u>not</u> to work for families and children

- and <u>only</u> to work for schools, and governors, and for Local Authorities

Parents, and their children, <u>cannot</u> get a fair hearing in this system.

The System is actively forcing us and our children out.

PART TWO

In Part 1, I spent time looking at the key players within mainstream schools:

- Teachers (and Head Teachers)
- TAs
- Heads
- Governors
- Local Authorities

The ideas and agreements that make the school relationship tick, including:

- Why we send our children to school
- Getting a child's needs recognised in a school
- The Social Contract
- The Early Years Foundation Stage
- Teacher's Standards
- Quality First Teaching
- School discipline policies

and how all those things might work for or against SEND families, and/or lead to "intelligence cleansing".

In Part 2, let's see how all these roles, responsibilities, agreements and relationships actually work out for our children (and us) on a real-life basis.

That way, I hope we can fully understand exactly how, and why, mainstream schools education break SEND children, ultimately forcing them out of a system that is meant to educate and protect them.

Teachers Are Teachers: They are <u>NOT</u> Diagnostic Professionals

As we have already explored, mainstream school governors, Heads, Teachers, Teaching Assistants, and even some SENCOs, **all know pretty much <u>nothing</u> about SEND**

In spite of what we have already learned about the "social contract", about Teacher's Standards, The Early Years Framework, and Quality First Teaching … the vast majority of education professionals:

- who spend their entire careers in a building full of young hearts and minds, with all the myriad needs and difficulties any of those children may be experiencing

- or the governors who govern our children's schools

- who will usually be the first people families turn to when they realise their children need help

- **receive virtually NO training about Special Educational Needs and Disabilities, <u>or the law</u> that surrounds them**

Not during their initial teacher or governor training.
Not when teachers achieve Newly Qualified Teacher status.
And unless they take the specific training to be a SENCO, possibly <u>never</u> during their time as an actual teacher.

To put that in context, the National Autistic Society's Education Report, published on 30th May 2023, showed that although
- 73% of autistic children are in mainstream schools
- **only 14% of secondary teachers have had more than half a day's training on autism**

(You can read that report in full at https://www.autism.org.uk/what-we-do/news/education-report-2023)

And yet, in spite of this lack of actual knowledge, there is an exceptionalist mindset which means many teachers and SENCOs - the ones I draw in my blog - firmly believe:

- being "in loco parentis" means <u>they</u> know what is best for every single child in their class

- "Command and Control", combined with Quality First Teaching = "successful education"

- "Successful education" is measured by what the school or teacher expects and requires – not what individual children actually need or can cope with

- Parents do not have to agree with the methods being used to educate or discipline their child: the power lies with the school to decide how to do both

- And teachers <u>do not</u> have to listen to what a parent is telling them about their own child, if that teacher happens to disagree

As a side note …

On the subject of SENCO training, if they were appointed before 2009, a SENCO did not need to have any additional training in order to become a SENCO. Imagine that! The one person in a school (sometimes the one person covering more than one school as a cost-cutting exercise), who is in charge of multiple different profiles of complex, and often undiagnosed needs, and who has lawful obligations to meet regarding those children .. having <u>no additional training whatsoever?</u>

At the time of writing this book, a SENCO can <u>still</u> be appointed to this vital role **before they have taken any additional training to prepare for it.**

(You can read more about the mandatory SENCO Qualification and how it's planned to change in 2024, here: https://www.gov.uk/government/publications/mandatory-qualification-for-sencos)

Even when SENCOs (or their team in a larger school) do receive SEND training, it is in danger of quickly going out of date because:

- Knowledge about SEND, and the number of children with identified needs, are both growing exponentially - much faster than schools (or Local Authorities) can keep up with

- Schools often rely on resources/training provided by their own LA, via their own, internal "business solutions" services, rather than using SEND-allied outside sources like IPSEA

- Primary schools in particular tend to rely on their own SEN Governors to provide training - and we've already explored the problems with that..!

  (It is also worth noting that because we now have access to professional-level training ourselves, **the knowledge experienced SEND parents have accrued is far outstripping what many teachers know** about our children's needs)

But as parents right at the very beginning of our journey, once we start to realise our child is not coping in school, and their distress is manifesting itself so clearly at home, we are faced with a very difficult task. We have to raise something we do not yet understand, which is deeply sensitive and personal, and often of a medical nature, about our increasingly unhappy/vulnerable child with someone:

- Who has a huge amount of control and influence over our child's life
- With whom we (as parents) have almost no relationship

- **But someone whom we <u>assume</u> knows more about SEND than we do**
- Whose input we usually <u>need</u> in order to start a diagnostic process for our child
- Who is not a diagnostic professional
- And who has most likely had no meaningful training in Special Educational Needs & Disabilities at all

And that's where the difficulty really begins. We trust that the professionals who teach our children **know everything they need to know about teaching children, <u>and</u> about Special Educational Needs**: what they look like, how they present, what effects they might have on a child, and how to support a child with them.

It takes a tremendous amount of trust and courage for a parent to describe to a teacher how our child had such a violent meltdown last night about school, that they threw their dinner across the room, or nearly ripped the bathroom door off, or physically threatened/hurt a member of the family, or smashed up their own bedroom, or tried to throw themselves down the stairs, or spent half the night screaming that they wanted to die. Or that this same child just sat outside the school sobbing and sobbing and sobbing...

But we do describe what's happening, because we need help. And we do it, because we are putting our trust in someone with some level of expertise.
We open up deeply painful and personal parts of our lives to the scrutiny and judgement of people in the hope of support .. **without realising these people don't actually understand <u>even the basics</u> of what we and our children are experiencing.**

Teachers, on the other hand, are used to being in absolute control in their classroom, and they are used to that "in loco parentis" relationship we discussed earlier, being unchallenged.

So, when they are faced with a parent telling them - the teacher – that:

- such violent meltdowns are happening at home

- and that the teacher might have missed something really fundamental about a child in their care, like a Special Educational Need or an unseen disability

rather than listening and wondering if maybe they *have* missed something, **far too many** TAs, teachers, SENCOs and senior leadership teams take on the idea that:

- because they spend so much time with the child in question, and
- because they do not know the child's parents at all, and
- because they are not seeing the behaviours and responses the parents are describing to them **in their classroom**
- then the parent must be getting something wrong about their child, and
- they (the teacher) must be the "reasonable parent" in this relationship

The thinking goes "This is not happening in my classroom, I am not seeing it. The child is fine whenever they are with me. So if the parents are saying this behaviour only happens when the child goes home, it must be a home problem."

Most teachers treat unmet SEND, and the resulting emotional distress the child is experiencing, as both a "parenting" problem, and a "behavioural" problem: never as a diagnostic or medical problem.

The result is, they will close ranks, turn on the parents (and sometimes also the child), blame the family, and try to make this "problem" go away.

Or at least make the problem go home - to where the teacher or SENCO is convinced it belongs.

The thinking goes: "How could a child who is so polite, compliant, smiley and regulated in the classroom *possibly* be "refusing" to attend?
Or going home and nearly wrecking the place?
Or waving a knife in someone's face?

Or punching holes in the wall?
And doing it because of a problem *in school?!*
Or because they need a neurodevelopmental assessment?
Don't be so silly mum and dad! Go home, be better parents, and sort out your child's behaviour!"

As we have already discussed, no matter what expectations may be placed upon them by Teacher's Standards, The EYFS, or even their own theory of Quality First Teaching ... **the absence of meaningful SEND training at any point during their careers, means the huge majority of teachers and TAs still know virtually nothing about SEND.**

And they definitely know nothing about masking, which we'll look at more in a moment.

Why This Matters For SEND Families – AND TEACHERS:

The important takeaways I would love parents AND teachers/TAs to get from this section are really very simple:

- **"School Refusal" does not exist. School distress and trauma does**
  - School distress (sometimes still referred to as EBSA – "Emotion Based School Avoidance" or EBSNA – "Emotion Based School Non-Attendance") is never about a child who **won't** attend school
  - And it is **not** about "avoidance" at all: **it is a survival response to emotional trauma**

- **It is never about a child who WON'T attend school: it is always about a child who no longer CAN attend school**
  - To diminish school distress down to terms like "avoidance" or "refusal" is to blame the child, and to abdicate responsibility

- **Unmet SEND, and resulting school distress, is not a "home problem" that is "caused" by "bad parenting", "lack of discipline", or "bad behaviour choices"**
  - School distress is a cry for help
  - When a family reports school distress to a teacher, what they desperately need is help and support
  - What they do NOT need is judgement, blame, punishment, shame, fines or prosecution

SEND is not caused by schools themselves
- o Any Special Educational Needs and/or Disabilities a child has, have been there since birth, and will be there for the rest of the child's life
- o But mainstream schools failing to meet children's needs, <u>does</u> cause those needs to present in a much more extreme way
- o When a child is too distressed to attend school, it is because whatever needs the child has have been **massively exacerbated** by that child feeling
  - unsupported
  - misunderstood
  - blamed
  - stressed/distressed by utterly unreasonable teaching expectations
  - or by their needs being dismissed/ignored in school
- o The environment around the child, and if/how their needs are met, make a critical difference to the child's life outcomes – but they do <u>not</u> create (or "cure") SEND

- **<u>No</u> family flags up a possibility of SEND, pursues a diagnosis, a neurodevelopmental assessment or an EHCP for their child just to "get attention", just to "have a badge", just "for a laugh", just to try to get our kids into an "expensive school", or just to make a teacher's life difficult**
  - o We do <u>not</u> want to be a war with our kids' schools
  - o But that is often how the situation ends up - and that is why so many SEND kids end up being "intelligence cleansed", forced out of mainstream schools with nowhere else to go

- **Special Educational Needs and Disabilities demand a diagnostic and/or medical intervention <u>as well</u> *as* an educational one**
  - o These issues are serious. And just like other medical conditions and disabilities, things like dyspraxia, autism, ADHD, Tourettes, PDA etc.,

need and deserve not just a diagnosis, but also treatments (where such treatments are available), <u>as well as</u> educational strategies

- As professionals, teachers, TAs and SENCOs have a unique opportunity to help a family, and maybe change the course of a child's life – **IF they have the knowledge and skills to make the right intervention at the right time**

- Parents are far more invested in learning about our own children's very real difficulties than the professionals are
  - When our child is in so much distress, and no-one is coming to help, we have to learn fast, and we have do so with very little support
  - **That does not make us "the enemy".** And it certainly doesn't mean we are wrong.
  - But it does mean our SEND knowledge quickly outstrips the knowledge of the professionals around us – and many professionals do not like that at all.

Teachers Really Do Know Nothing About Masking

Because of the rigorous demands Quality First Teaching places upon a child, and the strict behavioural and social controls schools employ, **masking is many children's only means of survival in the classroom**.

It was not a teacher or other education professional who introduced me to the concept of masking: it was other SEND parents. And once I started knowing more about it and exploring masking in terms of my own kids, I realised just how much my kids had to do it, and **just how little** some professionals actually knew about it or how it might present.

To give you an example, I was once told by a SEND professional that masking in children was really easy to spot. This person told me that masking basically meant if someone in the class laughed, the masking child would laugh too, to blend in. Or if someone threw a pencil across the room, the masking child would throw a pencil across the room too, to blend in.

This is a description of mirroring behaviour. Mirroring is not the same as masking at all.

Masking is mentally and physically exhausting. It's a constant fight for the child with their own body, brain, vestibular system, sensory system and a whole heap of other feelings and stimuli that are overwhelming, frightening, harmful, confusing, traumatic, often unbearable, and that feel like a threat to the child's very existence.

The masking child is trying supremely hard to fit in, to not stand out, and more importantly, to hold all their stims and tics and needs and panic and sensory overloads and everything else inside, to make sure that all those things can never be seen.

Masking is a survival strategy. And it is the reason why so many children who appear "fine in school", utterly melt down (or go into shutdown) at the end of a school day: **every moment in school has been a fight for survival.**

What I find utterly maddening about so many of the conversations I've had with teachers, TAs and then with SEND parents over the years is that people who really know what to look for, and who really understand the subtle tells of neurodivergent behaviour - even masking behaviour - instinctively know how to recognise it. Most SEND parents can spot another SEND family on sight! We have learned how! So it's actually not that difficult to see it **if you want to, and know what to really look for.** But most teachers / TAs, it seems, cannot.

So if a teacher or TA knows nothing about masking, or what it means, or how it really looks (compared to how professionals might <u>think</u> it looks, if they have ever even come across it as an idea), then of course they are going to overlook the child's difficulties or frame them as something else.

Why This Matters For SEND Families:

- Children with SEND - whether identified or not – often do not even know they are masking

- Masking is not a deception or a child "pretending"

- Masking is a distress response: an unconsciously constructed survival strategy

- It takes a huge amount of mental and emotional effort to keep the mask up all day

- SEND children who feel safe at home, will:
    o Mask their difficulties (i.e. "try very hard to 'look normal' ") in school
    o Unmask at home, where it is safe for their stims, tics, needs and/or distress to come out

- For a masking child to stop masking, there either needs to be
    o a very deep level of trust with the people around them, so it becomes safe to show how they really feel

    <u>or</u>

    o such a deep level of distress that the child can no longer keep their distress hidden

        o Unmasking is <u>not</u> safe in this situation, but the mask unravels anyway

- That means if a child is struggling in school/not coping with the demands and expectations being placed upon them (e.g. through a rigid discipline system, harsh uniform policy, and/or the rigorous/overbearing demands of QFT)
  - the teacher will <u>never</u> see the child in their fully unmasked, dysregulated or distressed state

  Unless..

  - Things get so bad, the child completely loses control / there is no other option left

  BUT

- If a child *does* become dysregulated / lose control of their emotions in school ...

It is far more likely to be treated as a "bad behaviour choice", **than as a sign that the child's survival strategy just failed**

If a teacher or TA knows nothing about masking, or what it means, or how it looks, then of course they are going to overlook the child's difficulties, and/or attempt to discredit the parents' version of events.

That's where the gaslighting of families tends to begin. I'll come to that in a moment, because gaslighting is such a massive part of thousands of SEND parents' everyday experiences within schools, it deserves a section all to itself.

As noted earlier, **no family <u>ever</u> pursues a SEND diagnosis or a neurodevelopmental assessment just for a laugh.** The process of getting these things is complicated, immensely demanding and emotionally draining beyond words. Each one is a massive commitment on the part of a family, because even just filling in the paperwork is a huge undertaking. The process is also often deeply upsetting as you are confronted in writing by what your child is actually dealing with day in and day out (the first application I filled out for Big Bruv to try to get him a Neurodevelopmental Assessment ran to more than 13 pages).

Sometimes even just getting your child accepted onto the (years long?) waiting list for diagnosis or treatment is like a fight to the death. So being on the receiving end of judgement, unhelpful comments and / or child and parent blame from a school, does nothing to make that process any easier.

And it is <u>not</u> a teacher's nor a school's job to voice an uninformed opinion on our parenting skills. <u>Especially</u> not when a parent has taken the vast leap of faith to bring this up with a teacher in the first place.

Yet if there is no behavioural problem to be <u>seen</u> in class - or one that cannot appear to be dealt with using traditional classroom methods (i.e. by forcing the child to mask) - then for many teachers, that's the end of that. Or to put it another way: **They. Are. Not. Seeing. It.**

After school...

But let's be clear: Teachers have no place trying to tell you what your child's needs may or may not be, nor how "severe" any needs a child has may or may not be, **when they don't actually know.**

Because as we have seen, **teachers are NOT diagnostic professionals.** And most, as we have also seen, know <u>nothing</u> about SEND, or about masking.

Why This Matters To SEND Families:

- **Special Educational Needs and Disabilities often need a** <u>**medical**</u> **intervention,** *as well as* an educational one

- An educator's job is to educate to the best of their ability, and within the framework of their professional standards.
  - **It** <u>**is NOT**</u> **their job to make medical or diagnostic decisions**

- A TA's, teacher's or a SENCO's job is to identify where a child may have Special Educational Needs
  - but as we have seen, many are not able to do that

- The teacher or educator becomes a "gatekeeper":
  - will they listen to the parents' concerns?
  - will they recognise that a child may be struggling with something **that is beyond their own expertise?**
  - will they open the door to The System with
    - a support plan (such as an Additional Needs Plan / My Support Plan)
    - and a timely referral to outside services?

- Too many times, the answer is NO: teachers, TAs and SENCOs <u>block</u> that door, because they think <u>they</u> know best

---

Blocking and Gaslighting Are The Default in Schools (and they happen to kids AND parents)

Human nature programs us to see the best in people, most of the time. We want to trust the professionals who work with our kids, and it helps us all if we can work together as a team to benefit our child. However, that basic human nature to trust can often be a SEND parent's worst enemy, **if we are not yet experienced enough to understand the system we are trying to co-operate with.**

School teams are, in my experience, very skilled at keeping parents in "silos". It's not unheard of, for example, for schools to "have a quiet word" with parents, and warn them off saying "anything bad" to other parents about the school or their child's experiences in it, if a child is struggling to attend and parents are not getting the help their child needs. I have also read schools complaints policies that explicitly forbid parents from discussing the school (e.g. on social media).

In doing so, and by keeping parents separate from each other, parents get no chance to speak to each other or compare theirs and their child's experiences. That way, schools can pretend to every family that's having difficulties with the school, that "no-one else is complaining, it's just you".

And that is a form of gaslighting.

The Oxford Language dictionary defines the word Gaslighting as follows:

> 'Manipulate (someone) using psychological methods into questioning their own sanity or powers of reasoning" (Source: https://languages.oup.com/google-dictionary-en/)

It's a strong term - but it's one I use from experience.

Blocking tactics and gaslighting in school usually comprise, in some form or another, of several well-worn phrases, each of them guaranteed to get an experienced SEND parent or advocate rolling their eyes (at best), or at worst, howling with despair and wanting to scoop someone's brain out with a spoon.

These phrases include (but are not limited to):

School stock phrase	What this really is
"Your child is fine in school"	Gaslighting: "Your child looks fine when they are with us / away from you … So it's not us, it's you"
"We are not seeing it"	Gaslighting: "It's not us, it's you" and/or "You are looking for things that are not there."
"Your child's educational attainment is fine"	Gaslighting: "Your child is meeting our academic targets, therefore your child cannot have Special Educational Needs". Which is a complete red herring: masking children are usually the most likely to "attain" against a school's measures, because they are so afraid to "fail" or be singled out / appear "different"
"It must be a home problem"	Gaslighting and parent blaming - shorthand for "It's not us, it's you" and/or "We are not seeing it"
"It's a behavioural problem"	Gaslighting, child shaming and parent blaming: "Your child is naughty" and/or "You are bad parents" / "We are not seeing it". See the next two points as well.
"Your child is	Gaslighting, child shaming and parent

being difficult"	blaming: "It's the kid's fault for not fitting in to our system" and/or "You must be very bad parents to be letting your child think this sort of behaviour is ok" In other words, "We are not seeing it".
"Your child is making some very poor behaviour choices"	Gaslighting, child blaming: "We can't handle the fact that your child is distressed by the school environment and is communicating that to us via their 'behaviour'. What they are doing is a choice. It is nothing to do with us. Please go away and teach your child better 'behaviour'." In other words, "We are not seeing it"
"Your child really needs to be more resilient"	Gaslighting, child blaming: "Your child really needs to make our lives easier / mask more / act less autistic / show fewer ADHD traits / just be less sensitive/stop being so needy/emotional" etc. Again, another form of "We are not seeing it".
"Your child needs to develop more tolerance"	Gaslighting, child blaming: "Your child really needs to mask more / stop having sensory issues / stop being "over-sensitive" / stop being so autistic/ADHD and just learn to cope in this environment" I have also heard of this being presented to a parent as "Your child can't deal with me shouting in the classroom because you clearly don't shout at your child enough at home."

	No. Words. (Except perhaps "We are not seeing it").
"Your child isn't an angel you know, they say some pretty mean stuff to other children"	Child blaming: "We don't recognise/accept your child has a disability that affects their communication and social interaction, or that your child may be lashing out verbally because they are in distress. Or that we ought to be doing something to help them. Your kid is just rude. That's your fault. Please go away and teach your child better manners" (You know the theme by now ..)
"What strategies do YOU think we should use?"	Blocking. Passive aggressive and definitely not proactive. Parents recognise their child's needs - they <u>do not</u> know about in-school strategies a professional and/or knowledgeable teacher **could** *or* **should** be employing: that's the teacher's / SENCO's job! Nor do most parents know what interventions could be done (e.g. Specialist outreach teachers), **because no-one ever tells them.**
"Your child's needs are not great enough for further investigation"	Blocking. Shorthand for "Although I am not a diagnostic or neurodiversity specialist, I'm making an assumption in my position as a teacher. Could also mean "I don't know what to

	do about your child's presentation, and I don't <u>want</u> to know what do about this because it sounds difficult / I don't understand the system." More likely to mean "I don't actually believe you. I think this is a behaviour problem. So I'm not going to do anything" See also "We are not seeing it" (above)
"There are other children with far greater needs than yours"	Blocking. Shorthand for "OMG if you think your kid is bad you should see some of the kids in this school…" Again, this person is not a diagnostic professional or a neurodiversity specialist. This type of phrase is an attempt to guilt-trip you into going away, and/or means "I've already got too much on my plate, I don't really know what to do, this sounds like a whole lot of paperwork for me, so I'm not going to do anything". (Often also coupled with: "We have xxx other pupils in this school, we can't just focus on one child you know …") In other words, "We are not seeing it"
"We can't treat your child any differently to the others"	Blocking. Often coupled with "Well if we treat your child any differently, they will <u>all</u> want what your child has. And that is not acceptable to us. Your child just needs

	to behave better/stop being so needy/show more resilience." A statement made by a teacher/TA – and often even SENCOs - who don't understand the very basics of SEND law or their own obligations under it - **i.e. that Reasonable Adjustments have to be made for SEND children by law.** Yet another version of "We are not seeing it"
"I have been teaching for xxx years, I know about SEND"	Blocking / gaslighting. This teacher may well have been teaching for many years, but they have not been teaching **this particular child with this particular presentation** for xxx years - and every SEND child's presentation is different. (Probably indicates this teacher has been missing the signs of SEND in many, many children over their xxx number of years as a teacher. Which is pretty disgusting when you think about it.) Yet one more version of "We are not seeing it."
"Let's wait and see if they grow out of it"	Blocking and gaslighting. "I don't agree with you that this may be a sign of unmet SEND. I think this is your child acting up." And/or "I don't want to have to do all the work involved in writing a support plan/referral

because I don't believe there is anything behind this other than bad behaviour".

In other words, "We are not seeing it."

This fails the child on so many counts: a SEND child does not outgrow autism, ADHD, dyspraxia/DCD etc. any more than a visually impaired child "grows out" of their visual impairment. Whilst growing, maturing, and having good strategies all help, it simply is not possible to just "grow out" of something that is a physiological and neurological fact that has been with the child since birth.

"Wait and see" is not a strategy for dealing with SEND. Yet many teachers treat it as if it is a strategy, **and as if they have an option to decide to do it.**

- o "Waiting to see" if the "behaviour" resolves itself is actually waiting to see if sufficient shaming, isolation or punishment will cause the child to "control their behaviour choice". (But as we have already established, having a neurological diversity/impairment, learning difficulty or disability is not a "behaviour choice")

- o "Wait and see" gives the child no support, no affirmation and no strategies to help them learn how to work with/overcome the very real difficulties they have

- o Instead, "wait and see" requires a

	child to mask <u>more</u> in school, so their "behaviour" - which has become more noticeable as a child's mask slips - will go back to being more manageable for the teacher/TA.
"We don't want to label a child"	Blocking - see above. One more version of "We are not seeing it." "We don't want to label" fails the child on so many counts. **And school discipline policies "label" children anyway!** • Labels like "naughty", "disruptive" or "lacking independence/lacking resilience" are negative; they do nothing whatsoever to help The assumption in this statement is that <u>all</u> labels are negative. BUT … • **The correct <u>diagnostic</u> labels such as "autistic", "dyslexic", or "child with ADHD" are really positive!** The correct <u>diagnostic </u>"label" helps a child to understand themselves better, and to access the services and support they need. Without the correct diagnostic label, the child gets no support, and the problems just keep getting bigger (resulting in yet more negative labels that do literally nothing to help)
"You and your child really need to focus on the	Gaslighting, misogyny and absolute parent blame.

positives in school, mum"	The most treacherous of all the versions of "We are not seeing it".
"You need to stop pushing this negative narrative about your child, mum"	Phrases like these are a veiled accusation of FII ("Fabricated or Induced Illness" – see below).
	Don't even get me started.
OR	
"Are you sure you're not just making your child more anxious, because you are anxious, mum ?"	
Also sometimes accompanied by:	
"We're starting to have a few safeguarding concerns.."	

If you come up against any of these phrases from people in your child's school or your LA, <u>know for sure</u> that you are being blocked and/or gaslighted. Many schools seem to believe the parents are "creating" issues around their child that aren't really there – either

- Because mum's a bit "over-emotional" / "over-invested" / "over-protective" / "too sensitive"

   OR

- in order to get attention.   This is known as FII ("Fabricated or Induced Illness" – formerly called "Munchausen's Syndrome By Proxy")

In its genuine form, FII is a method of child abuse and a mental illness which (according to the NHS website) causes the parent to deliberately exaggerate or invent symptoms, or deliberately make their child ill. The reasons for it are not well understood, but to quote the NHS website, it may happen:

> "... because the parent or carer gains something, such as attention, support or closeness to the child. Or it may be because they have anxiety or incorrect beliefs about their child's health, and they need these beliefs to be confirmed and acted upon. The parent or carer is not always fully aware of the reasons for their own behaviour".

(Source: https://www.nhs.uk/mental-health/conditions/fabricated-or-induced-illness/overview/)

Genuine cases of FII are exceptionally rare

Yet SEND parents are accused of FII, or told by schools that they have "safeguarding concerns" about the parents, with an alarming and almost casual regularity.

Let me be absolutely clear: Neither schools, nor LAs, have any right whatsoever to imply a parent is creating FII when those parents are actually speaking to a school about possible unmet SEND.

Falsely accusing SEND parents of being mentally ill/causing harm/abusing their child is the ultimate form of gaslighting.
Accusations like these - whether made openly or in a veiled form - are insidious, vicious weaponry deployed by a school (and often also by an LA), **directly designed to get the parents to doubt themselves and/or back off out of fear.**

Worse still, both male and female staff seem to have no problem targeting SEND **mums** with these psychological tactics:

- It is most usually the child's mum who is going to get the (so-called) "friendly chat" from a teacher at the end of a school day

145

- It is also most likely to be the child's mum who spends the most time in the school's or LA's face, once things start to go wrong for the child

My statements are not intended to blame SEND dads, by the way: the simple fact is, no matter which parent may travel the furthest for work, have the higher earning job, work the most hours, may not be in work, or even if parents are separated and have 50:50 custody, **it is still far more likely that a school will call on a child's mum first** whenever there is a problem, rather than the child's dad.

The problem gets even worse for lone SEND parents – many of whom are mums, and who may have no-one else in the family that they can call on for backup, once these tactics begin.

Gaslighting, misogyny and insinuations of FII are tactics that I, and many parents who engage with my blog, have experienced first hand. But to suggest a parent may be deliberately

- causing harm or anxiety to their child
- exaggerating their child's difficulties "just for effect"
- "infecting" their child with their own "hysteria"

and/or questioning the parents' mental health **takes a teacher's over-inflated idea of being "the reasonable parent" in the relationship, to its absolute and furthest extreme.**

These are deliberate attempts to erode, infantilise and undermine parents as credible advocates for their child.

These are tactics which must not be tolerated for a second.

Organisations like IPSEA, Special Needs Jungle and SOS!SEN (to name a few) now offer excellent resources about FII, so parents can arm themselves against this particular line of attack. It is definitely becoming a more common one from schools and LAs alike.

But whether schools stick with "we are not seeing it", throw in some casual misogyny, or go all the way off the scale to an accusation of FII, tactics like these waste precious time:

- Time when a referral could be working its way through the system
- Time when even basic support could be put in place, very quickly and easily and at minimal cost to the school, that would immediately begin to help your child

The reasons for these tactics are many and varied. It may be completely unconscious: perhaps the teacher *really does believe* they know enough about your child and their needs to make a judgement call.

But a teacher's belief is not the same as fact - and I'll say it again: teachers are not diagnostic professionals

When someone in your child's environment uses phrases like these, you can be absolutely sure they are not yours or your child's ally.

Instead, you are dealing with a "professional" (often, sadly, a whole school team which includes that professional) that needs approaching with extreme caution. That school team has closed down on you because they are so sure they are right – so by default you, the parent, are wrong.

The tactics I mentioned earlier, like emails going unanswered, meetings being declined, or conversations being made impossibly short to cut you off, will also be deployed.

And because the profession as a whole is not on the same page as parents .. and for all the reasons we have already discussed about

- the failure of the Early Years Framework to catch many SEND children
- The failure of Quality First Teaching to adapt to SEND
- "Command and Control" discipline

- ○ The culture of "We Know Best"
- ○ and all the other difficulties schools throw in the way of parents and children …

The school has now begun to employ "Command and Control" against you: as parents, you are being very "badly behaved", you are "making some very poor choices", and you are not following "the rules".

You are expected and/or required to obey the school, back off and shut up, or suffer the consequences - because "school knows best"

And if that doesn't work, then - either covertly or openly - the school will move inexorably towards a position of "Intelligence Cleansing".

- • You are causing too many problems for the school, and/or "upsetting staff"
- • The school has had quite enough of this nonsense and would now like it to stop
- • It is time for you to shut up, or leave
- • Or to put it another way, "Fit in, or F-off"

It's a sad truth that this situation is likely to come up many, many times during your child's school career, just as it has for LongRoadDad and I.

And as we have already discussed, changing schools just moves the problem of your child's unmet need to a new setting, leaving it to come roaring back again at some point in the future.

When, for all the same reasons, your child's next school is also "Not Seeing It".

Let's Talk About Additional Needs Plans, School Support Plans, EHCNAs & EHCPs

As I mentioned earlier, it's very important to note that although I use the term SEND as a catch-all for our children and their needs, Special Educational Needs <u>& Disabilities</u> are not necessarily the same thing:

- A child can have Special Educational Needs, without having a disability
- And a child can have a disability, without having Special Educational Needs

That distinction is important under the Law, because it is Special Educational Needs that drive the route towards an EHCP: **only children with Special Educational Needs qualify for an EHCP.**

A significant number of children with Special Educational Needs are (for a whole host of reasons) in a mainstream teacher's classroom. So what is the pathway that teacher should be following if or when those needs begin to present themselves?

The theory goes that there is an elevating scale of support for a child who is suspected of having Special Educational Needs:

- Step 1 is what is often referred to – depending on where you live - as an Additional Needs Plan (ANP)

- Step 2 is a School Support Plan (SSP) - also sometimes called a "My Support Plan" (MSP), depending on where you live

- Step 3 is an Educational, Health and Care Plan (EHCP)

As a side note: Some teachers/schools will use the word "waves" to describe this process. If they do, or if you see the word "waves" anywhere in a school's SEND policy, treat that with a great deal of caution: "Waves" is the word used to describe the stepped approach of Quality First Teaching – and as we have already explored, Quality First Teaching is <u>not</u> a SEND intervention!

Additional Needs Plans (ANPs)

An Additional Needs Plan basically says, "we can see this child is having some difficulties. Here is what we think those difficulties are, and here's what we plan to try in school to help."

The ANP will be written by the SENCO in consultation with the classroom teacher and the parents. The Plan will be shared with any staff in the school who work with the child - e.g. teachers and Teaching Assistants. It will describe what the child's emerging needs appear to be, and what strategies school staff think might help. For example, does the child need 1:1 reading practice? Do they need fidget toys or ear defenders? Do they need a colour-card system so they can show they need some help with something? Does the child need planned "time out" to take a short break / go to a quiet space / run round the playground?

Additional Needs Plans usually consist of a couple of pages of A4, and are not very detailed at all. That's usually because at this stage, no-one really has a clear idea of what's happening for the child or how much / why they are struggling in class. The theory goes that the ANP will be actioned, then reviewed 3 times across a school year. If, after 3 reviews, the child's needs have not been met by an ANP, the child should be elevated to a School Support Plan.

The problem my experience has taught me is that because
- teachers "do not want to label a child", they don't recognise SEND and/or they see special educational needs as a universally "bad thing"

- and because many teachers rely so heavily on Quality First Teaching **when Quality First Teaching isn't an actual SEND intervention at all**:

1. It is <u>very</u> difficult to get a teacher or SENCO to create an Additional Needs Plan anywhere near early enough: instead, the "wait and see" theory kicks in

2. ANPs are a "sticking plaster":
    o If a school accepts that the child needs an ANP, then that child <u>very probably</u> has undiagnosed Special Educational Needs, and may have an accompanying disability. So just issuing an ANP and expecting that to be that, is not enough!
    o A referral to Educational Psychology, Speech and Language, and/or Complex Communications Outreach ought to happen at this point. These services can help support the school to better understand and meet the child's needs
    o A child who needs an ANP should also be put on the Special Needs Register with the Local Authority

    BUT

3. Schools delay putting an ANP in place for so long, by the time the child gets one, **it's probably already too late for it to work.**

School Support Plans (SSPs)

The theory goes that once an ANP has had 3 reviews, if it's still not being seen to meet need, then the child should be elevated to a School Support Plan.

A School Support Plan is a longer and more detailed document. It is intended to spell out more clearly what the child's Special Educational Needs are, what's working, what's not, and where the support needs to go next.

I have heard of some staff referring to an SSP as an "un-funded EHCP": **this is not true.** A support plan written in school is a completely different document to an EHCP. It is not lawfully enforceable like an EHCP, and no-one in a school (or an LA) should ever refer to any kind of plan that is not an actual EHCP, in this way.

Let's be blunt: SENCOs tend not to like writing School Support Plans.

Mainly, they do not like them because writing a SSP is quite a lot of hard work for the SENCO.

Yes, I get it: Writing a 6 to 8 page document detailing a child's potential needs (all of which are probably still unassessed/undiagnosed - i.e. guesswork - at this stage) is a big undertaking.
Especially so if you have a lot of children in your school needing one.
And even more so, if you are insufficiently trained to understand what the child's presentation of difficulty in the classroom, which has probably got significantly worse during the lifespan of an ANP, might really mean:

- Autism? (a **protected disability** that also requires Special Educational Provision)
- ADHD? (a **protected disability** that requires Special Educational Provision)
- Dyslexia? (a **learning difficulty** that needs SEP)
- Dysgraphia? (a **learning difficulty** that needs SEP)
- Dyscalculia? (a **learning difficulty** that needs SEP)
- Dyspraxia / Developmental Co-ordination Disorder? (a **protected disability** that needs SEP)
- Tourettes? (a discrete **Special Educational Need**)
- PDA? (also a discrete **Special Educational Need**)
- Sensory integration difficulties? (that require SEP)

You get the picture.

Each of those and any number of other conditions - or any combination of them - needs a potentially different solution, because each child has a unique profile of needs. Undiagnosed SEND really is a potential minefield when TAs/teachers don't know what they are looking at!

"And I've got to write a document detailing all of that??" says the SENCO .. and promptly takes themselves off for a lie down with a cold flannel.

As I say, I get it: writing a 6-8 page document for every child in a school whose needs you probably don't really understand, are "not seeing", or just do have the vocabulary for, is a huge undertaking.

But that's not the point. The point is:

Co-ordinating Special Educational Needs provision is the SENCO's job

The other very important points we need to note are:

- The child should have already been flagged to the Local Authority via the Special Needs Register

- The child should also have been referred to outside specialist outreach services like a complex needs team or SALT or Educational Psychology. This should have happened when the ANP was put in place

    o If that happened, everyone should have a far clearer picture after 3 reviews of the Additional Needs Plan, of what the child's needs actually are

- But, again because of "wait and see", "not wanting to label a child", an over-reliance on Quality First Teaching as the answer to everything, and SENCOs/teachers being insufficiently trained to understand why these referrals matter so much ... the referrals are unlikely to have been made

- So, still, no-one really understands the child's needs

- And those needs are still not being met, no matter how many times the SSP is reviewed

- **So an SSP also has very little chance of actually working.**

By this stage, it's likely that the parents are becoming more and more upset, frustrated and fearful for their rapidly unravelling and increasingly distressed child. They are, after all, the ones who have to witness the emotional and mental health fallout these failures are creating for their child, and somehow deal with them at home - usually with no support whatsoever, because no-one else is "seeing it".

The child is probably finding it harder and harder to attend school. School Distress (formerly known as EBSA – "Emotion Based School Avoidance" or worse still "School Refusal") is establishing as the child's ability to attend school – or cope when they are there - becomes more and more fragmented.

The parents will probably now start to push for the child to be elevated to an Education, Health and Care Plan (EHCP), in the hope this will finally trigger the support their child so clearly needs.

And the school will most likely be pushing back against that, very very hard. Because the school's belief is still that the child is, overall, "fine in school". (Even if they have agreed to write any kind of support plan! Go figure!)

The problem for parents here is, teachers / school leaders have made a judgement that, whatever plan they have put in place, the child's "needs are not great enough for an EHCP" - **a judgement no teacher should ever make,** because as we have already discovered, teachers are not diagnostic professionals!

To put it another way, in spite of all the evidence from the family, and in spite of the child needing a support plan, the school are still "Not Seeing It".

Let's just pause for a moment ...

Before we look more closely at Needs Assessments, I'm going to take a brief detour into the realms of diagnosis.

- **It is <u>not</u> necessary for a child to have a formal diagnosis, for the correct Special Needs support to kick in.**

- It is also <u>not</u> necessary for a child to have any kind of formal diagnosis, in order for the Equality Act 2010 to apply to any disabilities that may accompany their Special Educational Needs.

- **It is, however, much easier to get the right support with the right diagnosis.**

But getting a diagnosis can be one of the longest and hardest fights parents ever face. One of the biggest difficulties is that although a diagnosis of autism or ADHD etc. is a **medical** process, in my local area at least, GPs have historically **not** been allowed to forward the child for diagnosis: the neurodevelopmental assessment referral has had to come from the child's school.

And with everything we have discussed so far, it is easy to see exactly why that's such a massive problem.

Like the fight to get an Additional Needs Plan or School Support Plan, the fight with a school just to get a diagnostic <u>referral</u> (never mind the diagnosis itself) can take years: years when a child's needs are still going unrecognised, still being left unmet, and the child's mental health is being severely impacted over and over again.

Then, after what can often feel like a fight to the death **just to get the school to refer**, once the child gets their referral the waiting list for assessment takes not weeks, or months, but <u>years</u>.

Although the NHS's own rules say no child should lawfully wait more than 18 weeks for a Neurodevelopmental Assessment, both Big Bruv and Little Sis had to wait for more than **18 months** to reach the top of the waiting list in our area.
And they were some of the luckier ones - I've heard from families in other parts of the country whose children have waited more than 5 years. Some children around the UK are on record as having to wait **10** years.
(Source: https://www.bbc.co.uk/news/articles/cn0d28zk1q8o)

While they wait, the majority of families will continue to be blocked and gaslighted by their child's school - simply <u>because</u> the child does not have a firm diagnosis - **even though a diagnosis is not actually needed,** in order for the child to be put on the Special Needs Register and/or for in-school support to be put in place.

What about once you reach the top of the waiting list and your child finally gets a diagnosis? Well, sadly, it isn't the end of anything. It's just the beginning of yet another fight, to go back to the school or Local Authority and get the actual support it's now (finally) evidenced that your child needs. **For most families, the end of the diagnostic process looks and feels like this:**

EHCNAs and The Myth of The Notional Budget

The theory in schools goes that once a School Support Plan has been reviewed 3 times, if the plan is still not working/the child is still not progressing, then - and only then - an Education, Health and Care Needs Assessment (EHCNA) should take place.

An EHCNA is the first step towards a child potentially being issued with an Education, Health & Care Plan (EHCP).

Councillors around the country from Kent to Warwickshire, as well as the DfE's own SEND Adviser Tony McArdle, are on record referring to an EHCP as if it is a "Golden Ticket" for parents to get "whatever they want". As many SEND parents can testify, the truth about EHCPs is very far from that cynical and reductive view.   Special Needs Jungle's Matt Keer discussed why Mr McArdle's comments are so toxic here: https://www.specialneedsjungle.com/why-the-dfes-send-adviser-tony-mcardle-is-wrong-wrong-wrong-matts-directors-cut/

Credit: SpecialNeedsJungle.com

For now though, let's stick with that first step of actually getting an EHC Needs Assessment.

EHCNAs happen far too late for far too many children.

Let me explain why.

When EHCPs replaced the old system of "Statements of Special Needs" the theory was that schools would meet children's Special Educational Needs via

- the Early Years Framework
- differentiated teaching and early/targeted interventions
- timely referrals to outside services such as healthcare, Speech & Language, Educational Psychology, Occupational Therapy, CAMHS etc.

Assumptions were made that ANPs, SSPs and in-school expertise would be sufficiently robust to meet the vast majority of Special Educational Needs within mainstream schools. Also under that system of thought, the vast majority of children should never need to be elevated as far as an EHCP because their needs would be adequately met by the school and healthcare systems around them.

But as we have already explored, for a million different reasons, that system does not work.

For a start, healthcare systems were never sufficiently funded to meet this new world order.

Secondly, constantly shifting education policy from successive governments, actual teaching practice, school policies, and theories like Quality First Teaching do not take account of the reality of Special Educational Needs. So SEND children start to fall through the cracks in The System very early on - with no plan in place to catch them – usually because their school are "Not Seeing It".

Additionally, many parents - and also mainstream teachers - are utterly unaware that as soon as a Local Authority is notified that a child may have Special Educational Needs, either

- via the child being placed on the Special Needs Register or
- via an EHC Needs Assessment request

then the Local Authority becomes lawfully responsible for meeting that child's Special Educational Needs. Not just the school anymore: The Local Authority - to whom the school is ultimately answerable, and who should then be making sure Special Educational Needs are being effectively and properly met by the school.

Too many schools, though, believe that it is they who get to decide whether a child should be on the Special Needs Register (or to use their word, with all its negative connotations: "labelled").

They also believe it is up to them to decide whether a child's needs are significant enough to require an EHC Needs Assessment. And because they are "Not Seeing It", many schools put huge barriers in the way of families who feel this step is a necessary one (even though those families are usually 100% right).

One of the biggest barriers school teams put up, is telling parents that in order to get more help for the child, the school **must "prove" they have spent £6,000 on meeting a SEND child's needs in their setting** – the so called "Notional Budget"

- <u>before</u> the LA will provide any further support, and/or
- before an EHCNA can take place

Schools tell this story to parents all the time, seemingly out of ignorance, but perhaps also sometimes in the hope that a misplaced fear (of possibly bankrupting a school, for example?) will encourage parents to back off from demanding more help for their child.

But this version of how the Notional Budget works, is simply not true!

The actual case is that the Local Authority must provide the school with a Notional Budget of £6,000 to meet the needs of a SEND child, **once it has been made aware of that child's needs** - because it is the LA that is ultimately responsible for providing Special Educational Needs support .. <u>and then for ensuring schools deliver it.</u>

Too many school teams misunderstand what the Notional Budget really is or how to access it – which suggests:

- LAs have done a pretty poor job of explaining to schools what their role in funding SEND provision actually is (in order to save money?)

- Schools have done a pretty poor job of finding out what the Notional Budget really is and how it works?

More cynically ..

- There is a tacit agreement between schools and LAs simply not to mention it (perhaps, say, to limit application numbers..?)

  Or

- An even more cynical view might perhaps be that LAs make a deliberate point of allowing schools to misunderstand what the lawful Notional Budget funding arrangement really is..?
  Especially now so many LAs are under so-called "Safety Valve" / "Delivering Better Value" agreements which they entered into with the last Government, and which deliberately (and unlawfully!) limited Council's ability to spend on SEND provision? I'll let you decide on that one.

It is my experience that even when they have been made aware of a child's Special Educational Needs, the relationship between LAs and schools is a distorted one that simply does not work in the child's favour: school leaders and LAs are just far too cosy with each other!
And that is a huge problem for us and our kids.
Local Authorities, in my experience, use this cosy relationship to defer their duty of special needs oversight to the schools themselves.
This then creates a situation where the school leaders quite like being left to their own devices, and so do not wish to rock the boat/draw too much attention to themselves (by, say, asking for a lot of money for SEND provision, or requesting lots of EHCNAs..?).

The result of this deferral is a blind spot: far too many LAs fail to provide the correct level of scrutiny to what schools are actually doing when it comes to SEND, because they are leaving schools to scrutinize themselves. If that genuine scrutiny existed, LAs would hold schools (especially Academies) to genuine account when it comes to delivering the help and support a child with Special Educational Needs is entitled to.

This is another reason why ANPs and SSPs are pretty much bound to fail for the child: LAs are simply not paying attention to them. So schools pay them no attention either.

There is absolutely no excuse for LAs to abdicate their duty to SEND children in this way

One more very important point is even if a school can be persuaded to make a request for an EHCNA, day after day, LAs up and down the country are (completely unlawfully!) denying those requests in their thousands.

The "bar" that states when an EHCNA is required, is actually and deliberately set very low.

There only has to be a <u>suspicion</u> of Special Educational Needs, in order for one to be lawfully requested, and LAs have no right whatsoever to deny the eyewatering numbers they routinely do. Yet every single day, ordinary families are forced into the judicial system via the First Tier Tribunal – because their LA refused a completely lawful request to carry out an EHC Needs Assessment.

Why This Matters for SEND Families

- EHC Needs Assessments can - and should - be carried out much, much earlier than they routinely are

- **A child does <u>not</u> need a formal diagnosis for an EHC Needs Assessment to happen**

- Yet day after day, teachers and TAs and SENCOs and Heads and Governors – AND LAs - all over the country are, either wilfully or through plain ignorance, telling parents the opposite

- If schools and LAs understood the reality, and routinely requested/approved early EHCNAs, that would mean:

- Everyone would have a clear picture of whether the child has any emerging Special Educational Needs (some may not!)
- If the child does have SEN, an early Needs Assessment would mean:
    - Meaningful help for the child whilst they wait the interminable length of time most have to wait for a formal diagnosis
    - There would also be evidence available that would help the diagnostic process, and give everyone an idea of where to look
    - Everyone would have an idea of what child's needs actually are, before trying to solve them

- The routine practice of schools simply denying, or "not seeing" children's needs would end

- The LA would be immediately aware of their obligation to meet any needs the child had

- The LA would be able to ensure the school had sufficient training, resources, **and funding** to do so
    - They would be saving themselves the hundreds of thousands of pounds spent every year on failed Tribunal cases!

- And if it were done early enough, an EHC Needs Assessment may not automatically need to result in a child eventually being issued with an EHC Plan at all
    - Because need would have been evidenced, recognised, and begun to have been met at a much earlier stage in the child's school career

That was how the system was originally designed to work!

But the case right now is very different, and families – and children - are paying a terrible price for that systematic failure.

To re-iterate:

- Under the law, a child's ANP and/or SSP <u>does not</u> have to have been reviewed 3 times before an EHCNA can take place
- A child does <u>not</u> need a formal diagnosis for an EHCNA to take place

- The school does <u>not</u> have to evidence spending £6,000 of its own budget, per SEND child, before an EHCNA can take place

- And although many schools routinely try to block a family's route to an EHCNA, a child's school does not actually need to be involved in the EHCNA application process at all

---

That last point is important. It is no longer unheard of for a child's parent or caregiver to apply for an EHC Needs Assessment because:

- The school would not
- Other plans like ANP / SSP are clearly not working
- The family cannot get a formal diagnosis (or often even a referral) for the child
- The child's needs continue to be unmet/the child's school distress is growing

    AND

- **There is no other option left to try to get help for the child**

Yet although it is a parent's lawful right to request an EHCNA, very few families know they have this right. And when they exercise it, it often has a very unfortunate side effect: it causes what may have already become a highly charged situation between the parents and the school, to just become even more of a hot mess:

- The school now feels criticised/undermined; their exceptionalist mindset, and their sense of being in charge/"being the reasonable parent" in the relationship has been questioned

- The school becomes increasingly hostile, and/or absents itself from the assessment process in protest

- The family are still unsupported, and still desperate for help for a struggling child, who is still registered at the school (that same school who just got seriously pissy about the EHCNA being requested without their "permission")

- Lo and behold, if/when it takes place, the Needs Assessment shows up some really significant needs that are now so far established, they are (most likely) inevitably going to need an EHCP in order to describe and meet them

- **But the school still is "Not Seeing It"**

As a side note, It is also worth pointing out that although parental requests make up a very small proportion of EHCNA requests, Local Authorities turn down **up to 96%** of parent applications. To quote a March 2024 article by Special Needs Jungle:

- LAs refuse most EHCNA requests from families: Just over half (50.8%) of requests from parents, carers or guardians were refused by 114 LAs in 2023. Overall, the people who were most likely to get refused were young people with SEND themselves (60.5%).

- Twenty-one of 114 LAs refused more than two-thirds of EHCNA requests from families in 2023. The highest refusal rate was in Windsor and Maidenhead, who refused 96% of requests from families. (Source: https://www.specialneedsjungle.com/ehc-needs-assessments-2023-asking-snj-foi-data-not-parents/)

I'm going to say this once more for absolute clarity: **No family ever applies for an EHCNA or tries to obtain an EHCP for their child "just for fun".** The processes alone are a rare kind of hell; which this sketch probably sums up:

What Dealing With EHCPs Feels Like...

© The Long Road

Big Bruv and Little Sis – like many SEND children – should, at least in theory, have been able to thrive in mainstream school.

If The System had worked as intended, their needs should have been identified, and met, via that system, at a much younger age.

If these things had happened, it is quite possible Big Bruv and Little Sis may never have needed an EHCP at all.

But The System that was supposed to see their needs, help and support them **failed** – resulting in years of misery, distress, and ultimately in completely shattered mental health for both children.

Their needs and distress became so great, the only hope they had left was an EHCP.

The fallout from these systematic failures has been devastating for both Big Bruv and Little Sis. It is fallout that we, as a family, are still trying to overcome.

We Need To Be Honest About Command & Control, And Everything Attached To It

I've used the phrase "Command & Control" quite a few times now. Let's give it a bit more attention, because it is such an important part of most children's school experience, yet very little notice seems to be given to its effects on thousands of children, both with and without SEND, and especially on those children with EHCPs.

I do get it: there are a heck of a lot more children in a school than there are teachers. Someone has to be in charge, somehow! **But Command and Control is not the same as genuine, people-focused leadership.** It is an approach that is no longer fit for purpose in our schools, if indeed it ever was.

Additionally, I'd go so far as to say **Command and Control is to SEND what matches are to petrol**: the two simply do not mix, and never should .. unless, that is, someone is deliberately trying to cause an explosion. That analogy will, I hope, explain itself as I go along.

As I mentioned earlier, the now almost-daily news stories of children "disappearing from school" / "ghost children" .. the vast numbers of parents having no option but to absent their child from school for the sake of their child's mental wellbeing .. All these things are telling us there is a huge problem in our mainstream schools.

I believe it stems from a toxic combination:

- A dearth of SEND knowledge and expertise
- The lack of early interventions (and the almost impossibility of getting them)
- The rigorous demands of Quality First Teaching
- "Command and Control" <u>gone out of control</u>

The historical hangovers I've described earlier regarding discipline and control in schools are, at their heart, psychological bullying. These practices are perpetuated in education policy after education policy, because ministers and educators have always seemed to have an unshakeable belief that "this sort of discipline never did me any harm". Such policies are seen as the only way to turn children into "well rounded" adults / employable employees. I'd go so far as to say there is a deep-rooted belief somewhere in the UK psyche that only shaming, punishment and, dare I say, outright cruelty are the only ways to turn children into supposedly well-rounded, well-educated and functional adults.

But what these systems of routine shaming and punishment actually do is de-humanise children. They see children as some homogenous blob with no thoughts or feelings of their own, treating them as second-class citizens with no autonomy, and no real right to physical or mental safety, until they become adults.
In other words, children in mainstream schools are subjected to a daily diet of coercive control, and state sanctioned bullying.

These policies are actively damaging the mental health and wellbeing of all school children, not just children with SEND.

As I mentioned earlier, when corporal punishment was finally outlawed in state schools in the mid-1980's, it only happened because parents took the case for the abolition of routine physical cruelty against children to Court.
Not politicians.
Not Local Authorities.
Not school governors, heads or teachers: Parents.
Parents who stood up for their kids and said "No more."

But even when the law changed, the thinking around discipline and behaviour in schools did not really adapt – because the people making the policy decisions still came from the same background, and still engaged in the same group-think.

As we have already discussed, although children were no longer receiving beatings or having things thrown at them, the view of what "bad behaviour" was, what drove it, and how to "stamp it out" remained the same.

Even now, in the 21st Century, the practice of quasi-military control, isolation, routine shaming and psychological punishment of children has not died out.

Worse still, education policy and the view of how children should be treated in school has hardened significantly in the last 30 years.

Successive Education Secretaries determined to put their own stamp on the Department for Education and on education policy as a whole, have made sure there has been an active push to "adultify" children, to enforce "independence" on them at the very earliest moment after they walk through the school gates. This is enforced long before many children are developmentally ready to be truly independent (within the very limited definition schools give to that word).

Some examples:
- Even small children are expected by teachers to pack their own bags, fasten their shoes, and make choices "independently" without any help from a parent or adult
- Disproportionate penalties are handed out for forgetting a pen or a ruler
- Even the youngest children get harried and hurried (and shamed) if they cannot get changed quickly enough for PE, or fasten their own coat at playtime
- Year 6 children are routinely told they are an "example to the rest of the school" (i.e. they must not behave in any way that makes them look like the children they actually still are)

I'd go further and say words like "independence" and "resilience" have been literally weaponised against children in schools - particularly against SEND children.

Here's a perfect real-life example, as shared with me by a SEND parent via my blog:

A child's (let's call them Sam) EHCP - a legally enforceable care plan, let's remember - states very clearly that because Sam has Special Educational Needs & Disabilities, they **need** full and dedicated 1:1 TA support in every lesson. Sam struggles to stay on task, struggles to process both auditory and visual information, and needs either a laptop/assistive tech or scribing support for writing. Yet Sam's parents found a postcard in their child's bag that was given to Sam by one of their teachers which said:

"Even though I was mean and made (name of TA) leave you alone, you smashed working independently and showed excellent resilience"

Let's unpick that for a second:

- a SEND child, with multiple and documented complex Special Educational Needs, has a legally enforceable plan that says they **need and must have** dedicated 1:1 TA support in all lessons, in order to support and enable their learning

- Yet Sam's teacher
  - The professional who is signed up to the mandatory Teacher's Standards
  - and who apparently is a "teacher of SEND because of Quality First Teaching"

- Decided to be (quote) "mean"
  - and make the TA leave Sam to work "independently"
  - i.e. without the very support Sam's Special Educational Needs & Disabilities mean they need

- The teacher did this to prove Sam can show (quote) "excellent resilience"

- Their actions

- ○ **Actively removed** the educational support a SEND child needs and is entitled to
- ○ <u>forced</u> **a SEND child to struggle unnecessarily**, to feel distressed, to be unable to ask for help, to not even be able to write (because they need a scribe) … and to mask all of those damaging things - in order to escape the shame of appearing to "fail" in front of their teacher

When Sam's parents showed that postcard to a friend who also happens to be a teacher, the only words they had to say about it were "That is <u>so</u> messed up .. What the hell is that teacher playing at?"

Well, that teacher was "playing at" what a heck of a lot of teachers are playing at with SEND children:

- attempting to force "independence" and prove "resilience" – even when Sam had a lawfully-enforceable document that stated what support they must have in order to learn

- when what they should actually be doing - both professionally and lawfully – is obeying a child's EHCP, obeying their own lawful Teacher's Standards, and supporting NEED

Sam's school were genuinely surprised when – for the 3rd time in their young years - Sam once again fell out of school with school-related distress and extreme anxiety, shortly after this incident. When Sam was still out of attendance many months later, the school staff were still declining to understand or accept what the problem with this teacher's behaviour actually was.

Government ministers, many of them from a private school background*, want to emulate the discipline systems they recognise from their own educations, and transpose them into the state school / Academy sector, **because they believe it's the correct thing to do.**

(* - In Prime Minister Rishi Sunak's first Cabinet formed in 2022 "65% went to private schools – over nine times the number in the general population – and 45% went to Oxbridge, more than double the average for all MPs." Source: https://www.itv.com/news/2022-10-26/majority-of-rishi-sunaks-new-cabinet-went-to-private-school)

Ideas like those of

- Katherine Birbalsingh, the previous government's former "Social Mobility Tsar", Head of the Michaela Community School, and proudly championed in certain parts of the media as "Britain's Strictest Head"

- The previous government's "Behaviour Tsar" Tom Bennett, who was quoted by The Guardian in 2020 as saying "Letting children off again and again is like a snooze alarm", and who described his approach to behaviour as "very low tolerance"

have been adopted widely across state schools in the UK.
Both Mr Bennett's & Ms Birbalsingh's ethos is that "zero tolerance" of any misdemeanour is the only way to train young people in how to be good students and good adults. The theories themselves may be sound (at least on paper); I'll let you decide on that. But it is mine and my children's experience that once those theories go through some school leaders' filters and get put into everyday practice, the result is so purist that there is not a shred of room left in these approaches for
- individuality
- differing needs
- different learning styles
- nurture
- or even a simple recognition of a child's humanity

There is certainly no room for even the tiniest act of rebellion on the child's part (such as not tucking in a shirt, for example..?)

Nor is there any room for a PDA profile. Or an autistic sense of justice. Or an ADHD need to move. Or a straightforward inability to cope with constant and unrelenting high pressure demand.

There is only inflexibility, and strictly enforced "discipline".

Just like the word "resilience", the word "discipline" has been corrupted and weaponised. The word "discipline" finds its roots in the word "disciple".

- The Collins Dictionary gives the following definition:
  "If you are someone's disciple, you are influenced by their teachings and try to follow their example."
  (Source: https://www.collinsdictionary.com/dictionary/english/disciple)

- The Cambridge Dictionary defines the word "disciple" as:
  "a person who believes in the ideas of a leader .. and tries to live according to those ideas" (Source: https://dictionary.cambridge.org/dictionary/english/disciple)

But what schools mean by "discipline" is actually "Command & Control"

Ministers and policy makers in successive governments have lapped these ideas up. School Governors, Heads, and particularly Academy chains, have embraced super-strict uniform policy and rigid disciplinary codes, <u>very</u> enthusiastically. Academies seem the most likely to have the hardest uniform policies (some even now refer to "business attire" rather than school uniform..) - policies which LA-controlled schools have then copied.

However, here is something to consider: LongRoadDad went to a school that had no uniform at all.

I went to a primary school that had a uniform in winter, but let us wear what we wanted in the summer. I then went on to a very well-regarded state high school that produced excellent exam results right across the board. What I was expected and allowed to wear then:

- generic white shirt
- generic black or navy skirt
- shoes - colour/style utterly unimportant
- sock colour - utterly unimportant
- coat colour - utterly unimportant
- make up - optional within reason
- earrings – what of it? (Yes, even during PE!)
- bag – who cares? Bring a carrier bag if you want to, as long as you are here

would *never* be accepted in my own children's high school today.

In fact my SEND kids would be in detention/isolation for *any* breach of their school's super-strict and proudly-vaunted uniform code, if they didn't have an EHCP that specifies relaxations in their dress code.

Yet even with that provision in their EHCPs, they are still regularly harangued by teachers literally shouting at them, day after day, for ties not being straight, collars not being buttoned, shirt not being tucked in, jumpers not being worn in specified parts of the building at the right time …

I've heard the reason behind this constant and overbearing strictness on dress code in schools is because "School is a workplace".

No it is not! Workplaces are full of <u>adults</u>; schools are full of <u>children</u>

Children do not "go to work": children are supposed to play, learn, and be innocent of the demands of a workplace. A child's only "job" is to be really good at being a child! And I don't mean that we should never encourage children to mature, to be independent, or to have autonomy or explore self-determination: we absolutely should do these things because that is how children learn and grow.

But literally putting a child in a cage, a place from which they cannot physically escape (as most school sites are nowadays in the name of "safeguarding"), and where they are not allowed any freedom, allowed any self expression, or even allowed to decide whether they are too hot on a summer day and take their own blazer off … is not how we encourage autonomy or independence.

Shouting at children, and discouraging all forms of independent thought except the ones the school deems fit, is not a way to develop independence or "resilience." I'd go so far as to say that what school policy makers really mean when they talk about "independence" and "resilience" is:

- "Learn to do exactly as I tell you, so automatically that I no longer have to tell you", and

- If you can't handle that, **look as if you can** until you are off the school site"

  Or in other words:

- **"Mask everything you think or feel as a human being.** It makes our lives easier, because it gives us absolute control"

But this system of control is a law of diminishing returns, which eventually only leads to a "winner" (the school) and a "loser" (the child), and which will inevitably distil down to one of three outcomes:

1. Kids who can comply, and who will learn to cover up/mask and tolerate the environment
2. Kids who will be unable to stand it, and who will rebel, resulting in "behavioural issues" the school will then attempt to "correct" through increasingly draconian punishment
3. Kids who will be unable to stand it, and who will be emotionally crushed, resulting in school distress and non-attendance

© The Long Road

The numbers of children in category 3 – emotionally crushed and no longer attending – is growing exponentially, and is no longer restricted just to those children with SEND: children's mental health is falling apart, and it is lazy supposition on the part of policy makers to still be blaming Covid for that.

The problems UK school-age children are having with their mental health were here long before the pandemic, and have been literally exploding ever after.
There is more than one way for children to gain independence and autonomy: barking orders at them to straighten a tie or show more "resilience", is not one of them. Neither is throwing them into the deep end and expecting them to just deal with it

.

There is a right time, and a wrong time, for all life skills to be learned, and the very best time to learn each one is whenever a child is ready. Command and Control, on a rigid timescale set only by a child's age/school year – rather than where the child is mentally, emotionally and developmentally ready - is not the right time.

Yet again and again, the belief amongst teachers, heads, governors, policy makers and Education Secretary after Education Secretary has been that "tough love" and / or extreme discipline in school "didn't do me any harm".

That's the problem: it did, and it does. But too many education "leaders", and too many politicians who have far too much influence over children's school lives, are too institutionalised to see the problem.

Command and Control is not empathic. It's really just a form of performative cruelty. It gives no room for even the slightest deviation, or any shred of actual humanity / personality. And it does not pick up on the subtleties of what might look like good old fashioned "bad behaviour" - but are actually either:

- a child, just being a child!

  or, more worryingly:

- the signs of a child who is not coping with the classroom environment because of, perhaps, undiagnosed ADHD, autism, DCD, PDA or sensory difficulties, *and whose mask is slipping*.

Some real life examples:

- Demi's teacher had a huge ball on their desk, of all the blutac they had taken off Demi - because "fidget toys are not allowed in my class" and "everyone would want some" if they let Demi have it. So Demi could look at the blutac, but wasn't allowed to have it. Demi was regularly told off for picking blutac off the walls around the school (because they really, really needed something to fiddle with and help them regulate their attention), and the ball on the teacher's desk got bigger and bigger as the school year went on

- Morgan would refuse to get pencils and books out of the tray at the start of the day. Morgan would often sit with their head on the desk, sigh, hum, or tap during lessons, because they either had not understood the task, or because attention difficulties made it impossible to stay on task. This resulted in Morgan frequently missing playtime, being told off and shamed for disturbing others by being put in the "rain cloud"

- Little Sis used to regularly sit under the table because she could not handle the noise and visual stimuli around her. This meant she couldn't finish her work on time. As a result, Little Sis was often punished by losing play time at break, and made to finish the work she had not been supported by anyone to do in class time. Yet her teacher (who was also the school SENCO) refused to accept that Little Sis was growing increasingly unhappy in their class. They also refused to accept that Little Sis was becoming more and more socially isolated, because she was missing out so many playtimes – or that being able to move away from the classroom at breaktime might have actually helped her concentration/helped her to regulate

- Big Bruv would make random shout-outs, or get up from his seat and start walking around the classroom because he was bored or frustrated. He was usually sanctioned for doing so, by having Dojo points taken away, being put in the "rain cloud", or having his name moved from the "smiley" side of the board to the "not smiley" side of the board

Were Demi, Morgan, Little Sis and Big Bruv being deliberately disruptive?

No - they were actually showing signs that they were not coping, and that they were no longer able to fully mask how they felt.

At different points in their primary school career, and at 2 different schools, each of my children had the school SENCO as their classroom teacher ... and both of those SENCOs told me (either by implication, or explicitly) that my child was "to blame" for being "difficult" or "disruptive" (or in Little Sis's case, "aloof"). Their behaviours were <u>never</u> seen as possible signs of something deeper. Because, after all, how could something so major as a Special Educational Need or Disability be present in their classroom without making itself known?

The problem IS making itself known. Because "behaviour is communication"

But as we have already discussed, too many TAs, teachers and SENCOs do not recognise masking behaviour at all.

They do not employ what their own Teachers Standards tell them they should be doing.

And the "Command and Control" techniques those educators have been taught to use so unquestioningly, are instead framing the child's "behaviour", as their mask slips, as

"Bad"
"Naughty"
"Disruptive"
"Aggressive"
"Unacceptable"
"Wrong"

Why This Matters For SEND Families:

- **Children are children**

  - Children are naturally good at directing themselves towards things that **actually interest and nourish them**. And just like adults, children also more than capable of zoning out the things that do not interest or nourish them.

- o **And most have no interest in a so-called "balanced curriculum"** – because who decides what "balance" looks like anyway? (Clue: it's not the kids!). Just like adults, kids would be able to engage far better with things that actually interest them

- o Children are learning about themselves, and the world, all the time. They have curious minds, and lots of different interests, loves, fascinations, individual quirks, strengths and weaknesses, needs, attention spans – and their levels of energy/attention can change throughout the day

- o They are <u>not</u> homogenous automata / drones / "mini-adults" attending a "workplace"

- • **Children have all the same complex emotional responses to pressure and stress that adults do.** Yet children are expected to respond to pressure and stress in school

    - o as if they are adults

    and worse still

    - o as if these things have no negative affect on them whatsoever

- • **Schools frame children's expressions of need as "behaviours" which require "discipline" - and punish accordingly using "Command and Control"**

- o I'll say it again because it bears repetition: "Behaviour is Communication"!

○ But school discipline policies make no allowance for what the child's behaviour may actually be communicating - e.g.: "I am stressed/scared/uncomfortable/struggling/unhappy and I cannot cope"

The child who's "acting up" in Y4, or who has become violently dysregulated by Y8, is at every stage of their school career seen as "making bad behaviour choices", that "need to be sanctioned"

They are <u>never</u> seen as a child whose needs have <u>failed</u> to be met by the adults in their school

---

Let's Take a Closer Look at School Discipline Policies: How The Psychological Elements of "Command & Control" Actually Work

As I mentioned earlier, if you look at most school discipline policies through a lens of Special Educational Needs & Disabilities, you'll see a lot to horrify you. Some examples might include:

Behaviour systems that openly demonstrate to everyone in the class who is "good"
- who can sit quietly in their chair
- who can give fixed eye contact / constant attention to their teacher
- who can do exactly as they are told, in the split second they are told it
- and who may well be masking

Versus who is "naughty"
- who makes shout-outs
- who gets up out of their seat
- who fidgets/taps/tics/stims

- and so quite possibly has undiagnosed sensory processing issues and/or ADHD that they <u>cannot</u> mask

Attendance charts that
- reward 100% attendance / punish anything less than 100% attendance
- show everyone in the class whose attendance is "good" and whose attendance is "poor", without taking any account whatsoever of <u>why</u> a SEND child's attendance is far more likely to be "poor" compared to that of their non-SEND peers. Factors such as:
  o Sensory overload
  o Emotional burnout
  o Crippling anxiety / EBSA / school distress
  o Mental health issues, for which the child and their family is likely to be receiving no help or support whatsoever

The awarding of a much-vaunted "Pen Licence"
- This is almost unattainable for a child whose handwriting is publicly deemed "not good enough"
- But the child who cannot write to a "satisfactory" standard by Y5 could well have undiagnosed Dysgraphia, Dyslexia and/or Developmental Co-Ordination Disorder/Dyspraxia

Strict uniform policies that demand absolute compliance:
- insisting on school-branded clothing, tailored skirts and trousers, a blazer, a buttoned-up collar and tie
- specifying whether a child can take off their jumper or blazer on a hot day
- specifying what colour, style and material of shoes a child must wear
- specifying what colour, style and sometimes even length a child's hair must be
- specifying what time of the year a child's parents are "allowed" to say their child could have their ears pierced
- specifying what colour socks a child must wear (even if they are hidden under trousers!)

- specifying what colour coat a child can wear and whether it can or cannot have a hood

These are clothing demands which:

- "Adultify" the child (again, "business attire", anyone?), but give the child <u>none</u> of the autonomy or freedom of expression an adult would actually have
- Make no accommodation for children with genuine sensory difficulties around heat/cold/texture/itchy seams and labels, tight fitting shoes etc
- Do not take a moment to consider whether a DCD/Dyspraxic child has the fine motor skills to fasten the buttons on their shirt, tie a tie, fasten shoe laces, or be able to change quickly enough before/after a PE lesson
- **Actively discriminate against girls, who are more likely to want their ears pierced, or are more likely to choose to wear a skirt:**

  o Girls are singled out, shamed and/or sanctioned for the length of their skirt more than any other item of school uniform!
  o This experience of being singled out / shamed for their clothing has a particularly devastating effect on autistic girls, who are

    ▪ highly likely to have an inward presentation (quieter, compliant, fawning), rather than an outward presentation (angry, fight rather than flight)

    ▪ pretty much certain to be masking

- and who are likely to deeply internalise that implied shame about themselves/their appearance, without even knowing they are doing it

A SEND kid's Guide to School Uniform...

Hair must be "tidy". Hats/hoods/cosy stuff not allowed...

Blazer I have to keep on all the time

Collar and tie that's uncomfy + too tight (+hard to do up)

Prickly jumper that I'm not allowed to take off without permisson

Skirt I hate the feel of

Trousers I can't fasten the button on (and that prickle my legs)

Shoes I can't tie the laces on / do buckles on.

They even tell me what colour socks to wear...

Hard leather shoes I wish I could take off in class cos I can't stop noticing them

©The Long Road

Detentions and isolations given to children who
- "fail" to keep to the uniform policy
- go against a school's one-way system
- are "disruptive" – e.g.: fidget, zone out, put their head on the desk, make sounds, "huff"/breathe too loudly, or make shout-outs (but who may have physical or verbal tics/stims they simply cannot control..?)

Suspensions or permanent exclusions metered out to children who:
- swear or are verbally aggressive
- storm out of classrooms
- throw furniture
- physically threaten teachers

- **BUT** who are highly likely have an undiagnosed SEND need that was never picked up earlier in their school life:

  - PDA profile?
  - Tourettes?
  - Sensory processing disorder?
  - In the grip of an autistic or ADHD meltdown?
  - Mental health issues?
  - But who's "fight or flight" stress response is being framed as "bad behaviour" or "aggression"?

Such strict demands on appearance, uniform and behaviour give Governors, Heads and policy makers a feeling of real control.

They are an easy sell to the outside world, because the received wisdom is "children need to be punished/disciplined". But these methods are not "discipline" in the truest sense of the word, because they do not teach and they do not guide: they command obeyance without question. **They are really just coercive, psychological and ableist bullying.**

To date, for example, there is no real, hard evidence that school uniforms make the slightest difference to social cohesion, feelings of belonging, feelings of safety, bullying prevention or children's academic attainment at all.

(Source: https://theconversation.com/school-uniforms-are-meant-to-foster-a-sense-of-belonging-and-raise-achievement-but-its-not-clear-that-they-do-197935)

Also, I mentioned earlier that the Education Act 2011 would give most parents the nightmares, if they knew what was actually contained in that newer Act, which now operates alongside the 1996 Education Act.

Just in case you'd never had time to look into this in any depth, here's a taster from Part 2, point 13 of the Government's own Explanatory Notes:

(Source: https://www.legislation.gov.uk/ukpga/2011/21/notes/division/3)

"This Part extends the power of members of staff at schools and further education institutions to search pupils without their consent for an item that has been, or is likely to be, used to commit an offence or cause injury to the pupil or another, or damage property, and to search for items banned under the school rules. It reforms the process for reviews of permanent exclusions. It also **repeals the duty on schools to give 24 hours' written notice of a detention to parents**, and the duty on all schools to enter into a behaviour and attendance partnership with other schools in their area."

To summarise some of the key points in Part 2:

- Schools no longer have to give parents notice of a detention: it can happen that day, with no notice at all

- Children can be searched, without consent, if a staff member says they have "reasonable" grounds to do so

- If a situation is deemed an "emergency" by the school, a staff member of the opposite sex can search a child's clothing without seeking either the child's or their parents' permission

- Teachers have the right to search devices such as a child's mobile phone, and then decide to confiscate it, dispose of it, or remove files from it. To quote the Act itself:

  o (6E) The person who seized the item may examine any data or files on the device, if the person thinks there is a good reason to do so.
  o (6F) Following an examination under subsection (6E), if the person has decided to return the item to its owner, retain it or dispose of it, the person may erase any data or files from the device if the person thinks there is a good reason to do so.
  (Source:
  https://www.legislation.gov.uk/ukpga/2011/21/pdfs/ukpga_20110021_en.pdf)

- And thanks to this Act, the only person schools now have to answer to directly for such actions is the Secretary of State for Education

Again, when you look at this legislation through the eyes of a parent - with or without a SEND child - the power imbalance that now exists between schools and families is very stark indeed.

- Thanks to this Act, a child has **even less** bodily autonomy than they had before.

- Their physical selves, and personal items such as their bags or their mobile phones, are no longer private **if a teacher decides they have "reasonable" grounds** to invade a child's personal space and belongings. No consent is needed.

- If the child were to react to such an assault on their autonomy – for example, if an autistic child was to become dysregulated/go into meltdown – the school can detain the child after school on the same day, and not have to explain that detention to the child's parents beforehand

- If a school decides to exclude a child, they do not have to explain or review their decision

So not only do our children have fewer rights: as parents, we also have fewer rights to know who in a school is doing what to our child, or why, than we previously did.

Is that what we signed up for when we first took on the "social contract" of sending our children to school? Somehow I doubt it. Yet schools wonder why parents are growing increasingly distrustful of the relationship between themselves and their child's school. Go figure.

Ableism Is a Thing

While we are examining Command and Control, it's really worth taking a small detour into the realms of ableism, simply because many of the demands Command and Control places on children in school are deeply ableist.

I'm really grateful to comedian Rosie Jones (www.rosiejonescomedy.com) for introducing me to this life-changing and life-affirming concept. Obviously, disability means uniquely different things to each disabled person: Rosie is experiencing disability through Cerebral Palsy, and her disability is not only a visible one, its one she actively *draws visibility to* with her amazing comedy. So her experience of ableism is unique to her - and perhaps very different from the experience someone with an invisible disability is probably having. But that doesn't mean ableism isn't happening to every single kid who is autistic, ADHD, PDA, Tourettes, Dyspraxic, has Sensory Processing Disorder etc., in every single mainstream school, all over the country.

Ableism is the exact opposite of disability awareness and inclusion

"Ableism looks like calling people 'inspiring' for navigating a system that is designed for exclusion, while doing nothing to hold the system accountable."

Credit: Chris Bonnello/Autistic Not Weird

Ableism is an ingrained assumption that everyone is (or ought to be) able to do all the same things as Everyone Else. And if they can't, then they ought to be *trying harder* to do all the same things as Everyone Else, so they appear to be more like Everyone Else (thereby making Everyone Else feel a bit more comfortable).

Rosie Jones first illustrated this message, and demonstrated how she herself had been buying-in to the idea of ableism, in 2021 on the Channel 4 TV show "The Last Leg".

Rosie had been working as a Special Reporter for the show at the Tokyo 2020 Olympics.   The heat of Japan, the filming schedules for the show, and the sheer distances she needed to cover to meet those schedules were making life pretty difficult for her; her Cerebral Palsy meant she was struggling to get around fast enough to meet her deadlines.   But she initially refused the offer of an electric wheelchair to help her get from one assignment to another quickly and with ease. She described her initial reaction as "I can walk! Why do I need a wheelchair?!"

But when she reflected on that, she realised she was buying into the idea of ableism.

And as a result, she was actually making her own life much harder ... just to show able-bodied people she was "really trying" to be like Everyone Else ... **instead of being her own, authentic disabled self.**

She then changed her mind, got an electric wheelchair, and she later brought it on the show to demonstrate what a huge difference it had made to how she did her job as a reporter (and how much fun she was having in it!)

Before seeing Rosie's piece on The Last Leg, I'd never considered this aspect of disability discrimination before. It never occurred to me that disabled people could be unconsciously buying-in to society's ingrained ableism too. It also never occurred to me that even our own ingrained and unconscious ableism was actually making life really tough for our SEND kids - without us ever meaning for that to happen.

And it made LongRoadDad and I realise that if we (as SEND parents) were doing the whole "ableism thing" without realising or ever meaning to, then lots of other people in our children's lives were doing it too: Everyone from teachers, to club or activity leaders, even members of our own extended families or friendship circles.

It made me realise just how little escape there is from ableism for far too many people with invisible disabilities.

So I did this sketch, because <u>every one</u> of these situations (plus far too many more to mention) has happened to my children.

© The Long Road

Ableism is <u>rampant</u> in mainstream schools

- Demanding that all children pay all their attention directly to the teacher at all times
- Demanding that children give eye-contact to the teacher at all times
- Demanding that children look at the whiteboard at all times

- Demanding that children do not fidget, or have any need to move without a teacher's express permission
- Demanding that autistic children re-phrase things they have said that teachers consider to be "rude"

All of these are deeply ableist demands, and are something that <u>many</u> children simply cannot manage.

So if the majority of kids cannot manage them, how do they stack up for neurodivergent kids, autistic kids, or kids with ADHD?

Would you, even as an adult, be able to meet those demands?

I'm guessing not. Yet they are **actively demanded** of children, every single day in school. Is there any wonder that so many children - with or without Special Educational Needs or Disabilities - struggle to accept such rigid demands in school, when they can clearly see no-one else in their world has to?

Even the school building can be a deeply ableist barrier to many SEND children – in spite of legislation such as the Equality Act 2010 demanding it should not be.

© The Long Road

I did that sketch on my blog last year to look at the barriers SEND children face, (both visible/physical and invisible barriers) and how children with invisible disabilities might be discriminated against.

It received a response that genuinely surprised me. I never expected for one moment that a parent of a child who uses a wheelchair would write to me, and tell me their child's mainstream school had knowingly timetabled their child for classes in a first floor classroom .. also knowing perfectly well that the school did not have a lift.

Open discrimination like this is simply NOT acceptable in the real world.

Every employer in the UK is obliged to obey the Equality Act 2010 and make reasonable adjustments for every disabled person in the workforce: the legal penalties for failing to do so in the workplace are potentially massive.

Many 21st century jobs are tech based, flexible, include an element of working from home, and so are, by default, really quite autonomous.

Additionally, the vast majority of modern businesses - those businesses our schools are supposedly creating the next generation of employees for - **are actively abandoning "Command and Control" management practices** in favour of people-led mentoring and genuinely skilled leadership.

- They are doing so because good business leaders understand the way to bring out the very best in an individual employee or a whole team, is to nurture each person's individual skills and strengths, and to treat people with respect

- Bullying or discrimination in the workplace is against the law, and HR departments exist to make sure employees are both doing their jobs, **and are treated lawfully, fairly and with dignity.** Disabilities and individual needs must be accommodated and adjusted for, by law

- Those same equality laws apply to schools too! **Yet you would <u>never</u> know it.**

    - If we really want to "adultify" children and call school a "work place", the <u>very least</u> we can do is apply the same lawful disability protections that exist for adults in the work place, to children in schools

- Many employers have abandoned suits, shirts and ties, in favour of more comfortable and practical items like polo shirts.

- Employers would certainly never measure the length of an employee's skirt, or force an employee to wear clothing they could not cope with because of their needs or disability

- **It would be <u>100% unlawful</u> to physically assault an adult and force them to come into the workplace - especially if the employee was in the grip of a mental health crisis**

That last point goes without saying, right? You would think so.

Physical Violence Is Still <u>Routinely Used</u> Against SEND Children in Mainstream Schools

That physical violence (or the fear of it), coupled with the psychological and coercive control children are under every day in their classroom, is driving an absolute collapse in children's mental health.

Every day around the country, distressed and traumatised <u>children</u> are being physically dragged into their school building by teaching or pastoral staff who firmly believe this "tough love" is the "right thing to do" to children with what are euphemistically referred to as "Attendance Difficulties" (or worse still, "School Refusal").

I have read many harrowing accounts sent to me via my blog, or posted on other SEND forums, which detail parents and children being left sobbing and distraught by the actions of teachers or school staff attempting to get a highly distressed child into school:

- Crying children being held in restraint by staff in school reception areas, to stop the child clinging on to their parent or running off site, whilst the parent is told to "just leave them with us"

- Children being assaulted by teachers and physically removed from cars, or dragged across car parks or playgrounds, to force them into school, even if the child is curled up in the footwell of the car or lays screaming on the ground

- Children being isolated/locked in closed rooms, sometimes for the entire school day, because the school staff have no other way of dealing with the child's "behaviour" ... but still insisting that the child must attend

- Teachers turning up at a child's house (sometimes with police officers in tow) to physically remove a child from their bedroom or home "safe space", and force them come to school – whilst parents are threatened with enforcement action, fines or possible imprisonment if they do not comply

These incidents happen even though a child is traumatised, and even when it is known the child is in the grip of a mental health crisis and/or extreme anxiety/school distress.

These stories are not urban myths: they happen with alarming regularity to SEND children right across the UK, and parents are sharing their stories in a whole host of SEND parenting forums.

As a caring society, is it ok to physically assault or restrain a child who is in a state of extreme distress and dysregulation, or who is in a mental health crisis, and is clearly communicating – in the only way they can - that they cannot cope with the environment they are being forced into?

Is it ok to use physical force to remove a distressed child from a car, or – worse still - from their own bedroom at home?

Is it ok to turn up at the family's front door with the police?

Is it ok for sometimes more than one adult to push or pull a highly anxious child through the door of a building they are actively trying to escape from?

Is it ok for school staff to assault or restrain a child in a public place, and/or in front of members of their family, allowing those family members no right of response?

Is it right to expect a family member, or other people who are witnessing this, to simply shrug and walk away, accepting the violence / physical control as if it is "normal"?

The answer to all these questions is "NO".

So that leads to another set of very serious questions:

- If we would not do these things to an adult in the workplace, never mind expect them to be ok about it...
- Why on earth would we expect a child – a person who has been assaulted, shamed in front of a school playground or car park, torn away from their parent/caregiver or safe space, restrained, dragged, then possibly isolated in a pod (sometimes even alone in a locked in a room) "for their safety" or to keep them "under control"- to then immediately calm down, stay put, sit still, do their work **or learn**, after such an appalling assault on their autonomy, their mind, and their physical body?

Yet all these things happen to SEND children.

It happens both to those children without a formal diagnosis or EHCP **and those with** a formal diagnosis or EHCP - in UK mainstream schools, on a daily basis.

And I have yet to come across any mainstream school or Academy chain or Local Authority that seems to be in any great rush to change that status quo.
Why?

Here's my opinion: just like teacher's leaders back in the 1980s were advising staff to "carry on caning", even as parents fought through the courts to have corporal punishment removed from the classroom .. so that same mentality of "children need and deserve to be punished" continues in the education profession to this day. And if that involves a physical assault on a child, even in front of their family, then so be it.

No.
No more.
It. <u>HAS</u>. To. Stop.

We MUST Talk About Mental Health

In recent years, several words have become inextricably linked in the media conversation when it comes to schools. The words I am referring to are "mental health", "teachers" and "OFSTED".

Before I go any further, I am aware I am treading some delicate ground here. So for absolute clarity, I am not saying it is ever right for inspection teams to put school staff under so much pressure it destroys their mental health.

OFSTED has been shown to be far from perfect as an organisation; it needed reform, and for reasons I'll come to in a moment, that reform is now beginning to be made. Historically, however, teachers, governors and school Heads have complained bitterly about OFSTED inspections being "unfair" or "too high pressured" or "overly punitive":

- o They have claimed that OFSTED only inspects on a very rigid set of measures, rather than viewing how the school operates as a whole
- o School leaders have said the stress OFSTED puts staff under is utterly unbearable - because no matter how hard the school may be trying, if OFSTED comes back with an arbitrary judgement of "Must Try Harder", there is nothing the school can do about it
- o If a school has been branded as inadequate / failing by OFSTED, it can end up in a doom-spiral of falling standards that the school cannot recover from
- o OFSTED has been blamed for "driving teachers out of the profession": staff fall by the wayside with stress and/or mental illness - or they leave to find a better school to work in

Does any of the above sound familiar?

It absolutely does to a SEND family.

In my view, the inspections many schools have undergone and subsequently complained about, have quite possibly given <u>bad</u> school leadership – the ones I draw in my blog - **their one and only taste of what school life is actually like, every single day, for a SEND child and their family:**

- Unrelenting pressure
- Impossible expectations
- Punitive systems that crush hope
- The only choice left being to leave

Basically, all the things I have spent this book talking about.

As for the good school leaders, the ones who have been holding out and pitching themselves against "The System", the ones who genuinely do care, and whose life's passion is only for the wellbeing, happiness and education of children no matter what OFSTED might have to say about that .. well, that pressure has proven, in extreme cases, to be devastating.

Please do not misunderstand me: I do not say any of the above to undermine the dreadful circumstances surrounding the death of head teacher Ruth Perry in 2023, and I feel it would be wrong of me not to address that terrible event if I am going to talk about mental health, teachers, schools and OFSTED.

We will never know (nor should we know) the full story behind such a deeply personal tragedy as that which happened to Ruth Perry. What is clear though from her inquest report, is that Ruth's life passion was indeed for the genuine care of the children in her school, and the pressure OFSTED put her under was unbearable for her. The Coroner's report stated:

> "The legal test I have to apply is whether I consider it is likely that the Ofsted inspection contributed more than minimally to Ruth's mental health deterioration and death. I found that it did contribute."

Ruth Perry's death was an appalling event that must never be repeated.

But I must also address here that what has been far less reported in the media, certainly at the time of writing, and which seems to receive far less consideration from unions/teachers' leaders and the press when they discuss mental health in schools ... **is how many <u>children</u> take their own lives, or experience the same contribution to "mental health deterioration and death"**, because of the constant state of pressure, fear, and trauma they experience under the bad school leadership I have spent this book talking about.

The mental health crisis amongst UK school-age children is real. It is terrifying. And it was happening long before Covid.

School-related distress and trauma is not that different to PTSD - but because the trauma is happening to <u>children</u>, **it is taken nowhere near as seriously as when it happens to adults.**

Children also have no union to advocate for them. **The only advocates children have are their parents**: those same parents who are routinely blocked and gaslighted by "The System", by Local Authorities and by mainstream schools, when we try to have our children's very real needs and very real distress, recognised and addressed.

In 2021, The Guardian reported that, according to a paper in the British Journal of Psychiatry

- about **7% of children have attempted suicide by the age of 17** and
- almost **one in four said they had self-harmed** in the previous year

(Source: https://www.theguardian.com/society/2021/feb/21/uk-17-year-olds-mental-health-crisis)

- The article went on:

> "The data, which is nationally representative, can be extrapolated to the UK population to give figures of **52,427** 17-year-olds having attempted suicide at some point in their lives and **170,744** having self-harmed in the previous 12 months before Covid hit."

These are absolutely horrifying statistics. What they don't tell us, is how many of those children and young people who have attempted to take their own lives or harm themselves have either diagnosed / unmet or undiagnosed Special Educational Needs & Disabilities. (I'll come back to this point in a moment.)

Nor do the statistics tell us how many of those children had EHCPs that **their schools actively chose to ignore**, as has happened to my own children, and to hundreds of other families who interact with my LongRoadSENDMum blog.

In April 2023, The House magazine published an article discussing the crisis in CAMHS (Child and Adolescent Mental Health Services) around the UK. Here's a quote from the article:

> "When one of her staff members stopped a teenager in the act of trying to take their own life at the supported housing unit she manages, Samantha* sought urgent psychiatric help.

> "I was told he didn't meet the threshold. Here was a 17-year-old with no family around him and a history of self-harm who had just been found trying to kill himself. When I asked what on earth the threshold was, I was told to stop being facetious," she said, incredulously. "It's almost impossible to get them the help they so desperately need."

It's a story former Children's Commissioner Anne Longfield says she has heard repeated by young people. "Even if young people attempt suicide, they are not automatically offered support," she said. "First there is a judgement of whether they actually meant it. For children in such pain to be told they are not believed is devastating and damaging but this is a reflection of the crisis in children and young people's mental health services. The threshold is so high because the system is buckling. It was struggling pre-Covid but the pandemic poured rocket fuel on it."

(**Source**: https://www.politicshome.com/thehouse/article/child-adolescent-mental-health-care-crisis)

And yet, day after day, both the underlying and the overt message that comes at us as parents is, if we would just stop being so "over-protective", leave the school staff to it, and force the child to attend, every minute of every school day

- <u>no matter how distressing that is for the child</u>
- and no matter how much harm it is actually causing them
- then the child would be "fine"

Because schools "know best".

And school is the "best" place for every child to be.

But that simply isn't true.

In November 2022 the Children's Commissioner published a report titled "Experiences of children with SEND: findings from a nationally representative survey".

The Executive Summary of that report states:

- More than 90% of all children thought that having good mental health would be important for their future happiness. However, only 75% of children with SEND were confident that they would have good mental health in 10 years' time, compared to 89% of children without SEND.

- Nearly 40% of children with SEND had an overall wellbeing rating indicating possible depression, twice as many as those without SEND.

- 52% of children without SEND said that they felt lonely at least some of the time compared to 68% of children with SEND.

- Children with SEND aged 16-17 were the most likely to feel lonely often or some of the time (45%), higher than children aged 8-11 (33%) and 12-15 with SEND (38%).

- Children with SEND were more likely to be affected by not knowing how to look after their mental health and not having someone to talk to when they felt worried or stressed (59% and 55% respectively) than children without SEND, only 38% of whom were affected by either of these things.

- The majority of children (90% of children with SEND, 94% of non-SEND children) felt that they could talk to their parents or friends if they felt worried or stressed, regardless of SEND status. However, children with SEND in mainstream school had a higher level of unmet need for formal support, than non-SEND children.

(Source: https://assets.childrenscommissioner.gov.uk/wpuploads/2022/11/Annex-4-March-2021-survey-findings.pdf)

To quote the young people's suicide prevention charity Papyrus:

"Over 200 teenagers are lost to suicide every year in the UK.

Children and young people suffer emotional distress in the same way as adults do, but sometimes struggle to know whether their feelings are normal or how to access help to manage them.

While there have been moves to prioritise the emotional health and mental wellbeing of children and young people in schools, many are still reluctant to talk specifically about suicide prevention. The stigma, silence and misconceptions around suicide mean that it is often not part of our normal conversation, and there is insufficient action to make suicide prevention training a priority for all who work with children and young people.

Children and young people spend a large part of their waking hours at school: teachers and school staff have the opportunity to recognise the signs that a student might be at risk of suicide and they are well placed to respond effectively. Despite this, many are unsure of what to do or say. Indeed, many are frightened that they may make things worse by talking to students about suicide. There is currently very little guidance for schools and college on how to prevent suicide and support those affected by it."
(Source: https://www.papyrus-uk.org/save-the-class/)

Additionally, Papyrus says:

"The number of autistic people dying by suicide year after year is a national scandal:
- 1 in 3 autistic people have experienced suicidal ideation and nearly 1 in 4 have attempted suicide
- Autistic people are 7 times more likely to die by suicide than non-autistic people
- Suicide is one of the main causes of death in autistic people." (Source: https://www.papyrus-uk.org/open-letter-24/)

To quote Papyrus's article again: "**Children and young people suffer emotional distress in the same way as adults do.**" As a society, we <u>must</u> engage with, and properly understand, the mental health harm the mainstream school system is currently doing to children – both to those with, and to those without (or those with undiagnosed) Special Educational Needs and/or Disabilities.

More and more SEND parents have had their eyes forced open to the level of their children's suffering. **And once you see it, you cannot unsee it.**

That is the moment parents of SEND children stop buying in to the idea that schools and teachers or The System "know best": they have shown us time and time again that they <u>don't</u>.

Clinical Psychologist Dr Naomi Fisher (https://www.naomifisher.co.uk/) writes in her books and on the Missing The Mark blog (illustrated by artist and fellow SEND author Eliza Fricker) about why the current approach to "discipline" in schools is so very harmful, and why thousands of children are now unable to attend school, every single day in the UK.

Organisations like Special Needs Jungle, IPSEA and SOS!SEN (amongst others) provide advocacy and professional-level, SEND-allied training to parents, along with a huge array of other parent-friendly services that help us understand what's really happening to our SEND children in mainstream schools.

Additionally:
- Steph Curtis (author of parent-friendly books about autism and PDA, and creator of "Steph's Two Girls" on Facebook)
- The "Not Fine In School" campaign
- Pete Wharmby (late-diagnosed autistic writer and speaker)
- The Nurture Programme
- Chris Bonnello (creator of "Autistic Not Weird")
- Myself as @LongRoadSENDMum
- and thousands of other parent-authors

write and blog about this massive issue on a daily basis. We write about our experiences, because we have all learned the hardest way possible: Children are falling apart under this rigid, and viciously punitive system. Children are proving that "Command and Control" – and mainstream education as a whole - does not work for our kids.

As a result, families like mine are leaving the mainstream system in our thousands:

- not because we wanted to
- not because we have any other way for our children to be educated

We are doing it because we, and our children, have had our hand forced by the sheer brutality at the heart of the UK mainstream school system.

But this crisis in education isn't just affecting our kids: SEND parents' physical and mental health is being destroyed too.

The only option parents are far too often left with – to leave mainstream education behind - is a decision the majority of families, like mine, **REALLY DO NOT want to have to make.**
It's a decision that leaves families with consequences which are both massive and life-changing – even more so when we consider that many SEND parents are highly likely to have unknown or undiagnosed SEND of their own. (It is only through my own children's experiences that I've come to realise I am autistic and/or ADHD too!)

The conversation we have with ourselves when we realise our child really can no longer attend school, goes a little bit like this:

- OK, so now I have removed them from school. They are at least safe at home. But what do we do now?

- How do I repair my shattered child? How do I help my child recover some semblance of their mental health? How do I help to unpick the years of trauma?

- How do I deal with extreme physical expressions of distress? Like rooms being trashed, doors being pulled off hinges, holes being punched in walls? What do I do if my kid starts attacking me, or a family member or a much loved pet? How do I handle my child telling me every day that they want to die? What do I do if my child tries to throw themselves down the stairs? Or runs out of the house in the middle of the night? Or finds a blade somewhere (even when I've hidden all the knives), and starts to cut themselves? What do I do if my child never sleeps, because they can't stop re-living their trauma? Or if my child can't stop screaming, just to express their emotional pain?

- How do I do this? When I am not a mental health professional, and there are none coming to help? How do we move beyond this crisis, when there is literally NO support - for them or for me?

- How does my child now access education?

- How do I teach a child with really specific Special Educational Needs that I, as a parent, have no real understanding of? What resources do I use? What strategies do we need? How do we do this, now The System has washed its hands of us?

- How do I get any financial help, when my kids' SEND funding went to their school, but there is no funding coming for me to help me educate them at home?

- How does my child access any qualifications? Or those supposedly-all-important GCSEs?

- What does their future now look like?

- What does my future now look like?

- What if I have illnesses or disabilities of my own?

- After years of fighting this system and having my own physical and mental health destroyed, how do I recover enough to help my child recover?

- If I have a shattered and vulnerable child at home, needing my constant support or who cannot be left alone for any length of time for their own safety ... and they cannot cope with anyone else in the house but me .. how do I carry on with my own life?

- How do I carry on working?

- What does this mean for our family's household income?

- What if we lose a wage and we can't afford our bills any more?

- What if we lose our home?

- What if I am already at breaking point myself?

- ## What if we just can't do this?

These are the questions no-one in the education system, or in any Local Council, is asking themselves

Instead, the single question they tend to focus on is:

"How do we make this complaining parent shut up, go away and leave us alone?"

This impact on parents, as well as children, is not a new one. All the way back in 2019, Special Needs Jungle published an article entitled "Children with SEND & the emotional impact on parents". In that article, researchers John Holland and Gabriella Pell wrote:

"Parents often described themselves as being under 'constant stress', this mixed with the grief of being in a situation that they had not envisaged.

Mental health issues were often raised as parents tried to negotiate through the challenges of the system whilst suffering the 'loss' of the child they had expected.

This had an impact on some parent's sense of identity and was described as detrimental to both their social life, as they had less free time, they were tired, and additionally, family and friends were sometimes not as supportive as parent's had expected." **Source:** https://www.specialneedsjungle.com/children-send-emotional-impact-parents/

That impact on parental mental health has only grown worse, as the mainstream education system, and the LAs that are meant to support SEND children, have become more and more hostile towards SEND families.

In July 2024, academics from The University of Leeds School of Law, the mental health charity Cerebra, The University of Kent's Tizard Centre and the CBF (Challenging Behaviour Foundation) held a collaborative conference to look at practical solutions for families "traumatised by the inadequate or deficient responses they receive from organisations, public bodies and services." (Source: https://essl.leeds.ac.uk/law/news/article/1978/addressing-systems-generated-trauma-a-collaborative-conference)

The term they used for this ongoing experience is **Systems Generated Trauma.** It's a trauma that most parents are experiencing – and masking - every day of their lives.

© The Long Road / Long Road SEND Mum

As one participant at the conference, a SEND parent and grandparent named as Donna K put it:

"As a parent and grandparent, having over 30 years' experience of both fighting and navigating the system for support for Education, Health and Social Care services, for my disabled family members, and supporting other parent/carers of disabled young people, I can honestly say that it has been a harrowing experience at times, leaving myself and other parent/carers feeling absolute despair and traumatised by the battle that they have endured and the constant firefighting to prove that the support is necessary and that you are not at fault.

"This leads to distrust of all agencies and professionals who should be supportive, along with every aspect of your health and being, emotionally and physically shattered. You have no choice but to continue to 'work' with these people who you feel have totally disrespected and emotionally abused you."

Also in July 2024, Birmingham University released the first dedicated study of suicide risk in parent carers.

That research showed:

- **more than 41% of parents with disabled children have thought about suicide**
- One in 12 of the 750 parents surveyed said they had made a plan to kill themselves, and some had attempted to take their own life
- But only half of those who had thought about suicide had ever told anyone or sought help (Source: www.birmingham.ac.uk/news/2024/more-than-40-of-parents-with-disabled-children-have-thought-about-suicide-study)

To quote the research paper's press release:

"The research, funded by the National Institute for Health and Care Research (NIHR) and led by Associate Professor Siobhan O'Dwyer from the University of Birmingham, was conducted in partnership with parent carers and has been published in the journal *Archives in Suicide Research*.

Dr O'Dwyer says: "Many people will be shocked to hear that more than 40% of parent carers have thought about killing themselves. But what's really shocking is that so many parent carers have been feeling this way and nobody has known until now. Parents of disabled children, and children with serious illnesses, are the hardest working, most dedicated people I know. But so much of what they do goes unseen, and they have to battle constantly with a system that has little interest in supporting them or their children."

More than 800,000 children in the UK have disabilities or long-term illnesses and the majority are cared for by their parents (who are known as parent carers). Previous studies have shown that, as a group, parent carers experience high rates of physical and mental illness, social isolation, relationship breakdown and financial distress, but this is the first time parent carers in the UK have been asked about thoughts of suicide."

Why This Matters for SEND Families:

- **Systems Generated Trauma is real.** It is affecting thousands of SEND parents like me, like LongRoadDad, and like you

- Yet our trauma, and the emotional abuse piled upon us by mainstream schools, LAs and inadequate health and mental health services **receive no recognition whatsoever.**

- When mainstream school fails our children, it fails us as parents too. We are traumatised for years on end, by our experiences of The System – just as much as our children are traumatised by their experiences in mainstream schools

- The school heads and governors .. the teachers .. the SENCOs .. the council employees .. all of the people who forced the decision on a family to fight a system 100% built against us, and/or remove our child from mainstream education, **have literally no idea of (or genuine care for) the scale of the impact their failures have:**

  o on us as human beings
  o on our lives
  o on our employability
  o on our finances
  o on our health or our mental health

- And they have no care for what happens to us or our children next, once their actions (or inactions) have successfully bullied families like ours out of "their" mainstream system.

- They all get to keep their jobs, their futures, their wellbeing, and their certainty that it is absolutely OK to keep on treating children and families in this way.

- Because, after all, who is going to stop them?

So, What Does The Future Look Like?

As we have more than established throughout this book, care and nurture of children's mental health and wellbeing - whether children have SEND or not - is not built into the DNA of the mainstream education system.

Care and nurture have also not been built into our system of government for decades, nor into the hearts and minds of generations of policy makers who have directed ours and our children's school lives.

Certainly in the UK, there has always seemed to be an historic, underlying assumption that the things "society" deems as "good" (i.e. good character, good discipline, a good education, resilience, employability, determination to succeed and so on) **only** come about through some form of cruelty or punishment - never (so the thinking goes) through understanding, nurture, genuine leadership or kindness.

It is worth reiterating that I wrote the majority of this book before the 2024 General Election. It is also worth noting that, before the election at least, the then government-in-waiting had not shown many signs that it intended to make huge or radical changes to education policy, to enforcement policy around attendance, to school budgets, or to the way the relationship between mainstream schools and families operates. For many SEND parents, that apparent lack of appetite for a change in policy or direction was worrying to say the least – but at articles like this one are now also beginning appear:

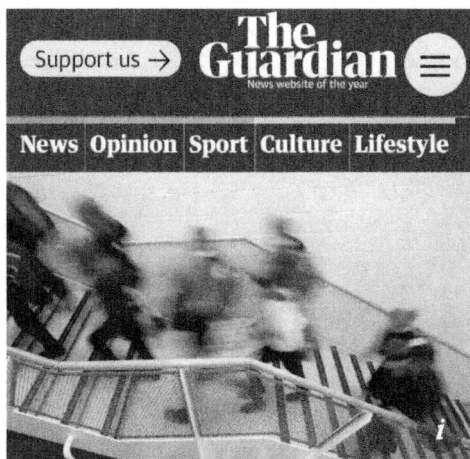

Schools

English schools to phase out 'cruel' behaviour rules as Labour plans major education changes

(Source:https://www.theguardian.com/education/article/2024/jul/20/english-schools-to-phase-out-cruel-behaviour-rules-as-labour-plans-major-education-changes)

Articles like this offer SEND families a glimmer of hope. Because, in spite of what *some* UK politicians might like to believe, it is not "namby pamby pearl clutching wokery" (to borrow a phrase from a current, more right-leaning MP) for parents to demand that the people in power **care about children's education, mental health and wellbeing** - especially when it comes to the education, mental health and wellbeing of children with Special Educational Needs and/or Disabilities.

As we have already explored, these are some of the most vulnerable children in our society. Children with Special Educational Needs and/or Disabilities, ADHD kids, autistic kids, young people with PDA and other neurodivergences are more likely to suffer mental health issues, or to cause harm to themselves, and to die early, than just about any other group. And once you know that, you cannot un-know it. We can never afford to close our eyes to that truth **even when The System around us tries to.**

If we, as parents

- no longer buy into the state-sanctioned cruelty that too many of our children face in the mainstream education system

- choose to no longer buy into the idea that authoritarianism, bullying, harassment, physical violence, gaslighting, psychological punishment and routine shaming are the only way to build "good character" or "resilience" or "determination", or indeed to educate our children

- decide to call out the staggering degrees of unlawful behaviours happening around us, along with the absolute dearth of accountability ...

then The System decides that we - as parents, and particularly if we are mums - are somehow to "blame".

The thinking goes that we do not have sufficient "moral fibre", or we have not built sufficient "resilience" into our children. I **refute that idea, and I am sick to my back teeth of parent blame.** LongRoadDad and I have <u>never</u> failed our children. But The System has done, time and time again, and it continues to fail them to this day.

As parents, we have one fundamental job: That job is to protect our children from harm

The mainstream education system has made it abundantly clear for far too long, that it does not want any child or parent who chooses not to fit into its strictures, to remain within the mainstream system. So the mainstream education system has actively bullied SEND families and SEND children out.

And when that is happening to you and your family ..

- When you, as a parent, have come at this problem from every imaginable angle ...

- When you have exhausted every avenue from TAs, to teachers, to SENCOs, to school heads, to governors, to your local councillors, to your local SEN commissioning team, to council Service Directors, to your local Council Leader and Chief Executive, to your MP, to the Department for Education, to THE LAW via a solicitor, the SEND Tribunal or Judicial Review (if you ever had the financial means to get that far..)

- **And you still cannot stop the harm that is being unlawfully caused** to your child in the name of "attendance" and "education"..

- What choice do you have left, except to remove your child from that harm?

- And then to fight to stop it happening again?

SEND law, for all its robustness, is only any good if families have the means to actually and meaningfully enforce it - which the majority of us don't. So it is time for a radical re-think, right across the board.

What follows is my LongRoadSENDMum manifesto.

© The Long Road

LongRoadSENDMum's Manifesto

"The System" is not broken – the truth is far worse than that
- There is a professional culture surrounding SEND that has gone rotten:
  o the culture in mainstream education
  o the culture in LAs

- Good education - one that meets need for all children – **requires will and costs money**

- Good SEND provision that meets actual need **requires will and costs money**

- Yet over decades in the UK
  o Successive Governments repeatedly used education as a political tool
  o Successive Governments deliberately throttled spending on, and investment in, education and SEND provision
  o Successive Education Secretaries meddled with education policy, without really understanding the implications – either for school age children, or under the law

- These have been **deliberate political decisions**

- Local Authorities, and the schools under their jurisdiction, have also repeatedly failed to understand their own lawful commitments when it comes to Education and SEND

- So LAs have:
  o failed to ensure schools uphold their lawful commitments to SEND children

- ○ <u>failed</u> to correctly train their own staff – either in SEND or in the law
- ○ <u>failed</u> to understand that they **must** provide the services SEND families are lawfully entitled to. None of it is optional!
- ○ <u>failed</u> to demand the money they needed from central Government, in order to meet all of these lawful commitments

○ LA officers have <u>failed</u> to ask the right questions when parents have begun to challenge them

○ Elected councillors, council leaders and executives also <u>fail</u> to ask the right questions – even when clear and unlawful failings are brought to their attention

○ And schools routinely do the same:
  - ▪ Heads, SENCOs, Governors and senior leaders all try to force the blame onto children, onto parents, onto <u>anyone</u> but themselves and their own failings

Education policy, and the profession itself, must adapt, change, modernise and outgrow its 19th century roots

- • Education is about children: young human beings, with just as many complex responses to positivity, fun and enjoyment, **or to an atmosphere of fear, stress and anxiety,** as any other human being
  - ○ Authoritarian, cruel, punishment-based, "Command & Control", testing and the competitive, league table-dominated culture in UK education <u>all have to go</u>

  - ○ So does political dogma, and interference from Education Secretary after Education Secretary, with no thought for the consequences on children

- Whatever the reasons teacher recruitment and retention are at an all-time low (and there are many reasons), the result is driving not just a lack of quality; it is also driving a **lack of compassion and humanity**

  o It means some of the teachers and school leaders who are left in the profession, are there for completely the wrong reasons

  o As another parent rather scathingly described it to me: "If all the really human teachers leave because they hate what teaching has become, the only ones left are after the pension, or they're bullies and psychopaths."

  o That's how real SEND parents really feel. **That is The System's failure: not ours.**

It is time to normalise SEND in the mainstream classroom
- Because SEND children are not "abnormal"!
  o They are just children in need of a greater level of understanding and support

- Mainstream schools have to stop shrugging their shoulders and saying "Not our problem. We are not a special school."
  o Teachers Standard #5 says teachers **must adapt their teaching** to meet the needs of every child. No questions!

- Stop treating SEND as if it is a "label" to be ashamed of, or something to be whispered in corners – or worse still, used as a threat

"Quality First Teaching" is <u>NOT</u> a SEND intervention
- Schools, teachers, AND Local Authority commissioning officers MUST ALL STOP pretending it is!

SEND is not a "behaviour choice"!

- Right now, it is quite possible (and surprisingly common) for **a child to reach high school age** before anyone realises they have been struggling with an unidentified, and therefore unmet, learning difficulty, special educational need, or invisible disability

- That is shameful on the part of the education profession, and LAs, who are all meant to protect these children

- It is also a terrible waste of opportunity, of learning, of wellbeing and of a child's young life

- If every child from Reception onwards was just given fidget toys, coloured reading overlays, assistive tech, adapted pens/pencils, "mushigrips" on rulers, ear defenders, wobble boards, footrests, access to sensory equipment, freedom to move

- Plus some other really basic adaptations like:
  - stopping the demand that children actively show unwavering attention to every word a teacher says
  - stopping the demand for children to sit still, stare at the whiteboard and never so much as move
  - just relaxing uniform policies and allowing children to feel comfortable
  - just being more human about "toilet access" policies
  - just allowing children to have crisps in their lunch bag, or juice in their drinks bottles (so those with sensory issues can actually eat or drink something during the day!)
  - just starting with the assumption from day 1 that some of the children in that classroom DO

have Special Educational Needs and/or Disabilities that have not yet been discovered

- <u>None</u> of these things would cost schools pretty much <u>anything</u>!

- <u>None</u> of these things would cause the sky to fall in!

- Yet they would have two really profound effects:

  o Children who <u>need</u> all those adaptations would never be seen as "weird" or "other", or get picked on, because <u>every</u> child would have them as standard from the very first day in school

  o It would be really obvious, really early, which children needed those adaptations most – and those children could quickly be screened for dyslexia, dysgraphia, dyscalculia, autism, ADHD, dyspraxia and loads of other special educational needs and/or disabilities <u>before they became "an issue</u> " in later Key Stages

- That is not to "dumb down" classrooms (as I have heard some people disparagingly state about meeting SEND needs en masse)

  o Because SEND kids <u>are not</u> dumb, stupid, uneducable, or any of the other assumptions 19th Century thinking places on them

- Nor is it to ask mainstream schools to become the "special schools" so many of them love to tell SEND parents they are not (as if that is somehow a bad or demeaning thing)

  o SEND kids are likely to be some of the most eager, enthusiastic, engaging, interested and interesting learners in the class <u>if and when their needs are met</u>

- Best SEND practice is actually beneficial for <u>all</u> children:
  - o It often just about doing the basics, and doing them well
  - o When that happens, <u>every</u> child wins!

So this is <u>not just</u> about funding

- Without doubt, there is a decades-old crisis in education and SEND funding. But that's not the whole story

- As we've already seen, many nurturing and positive interventions cost next to, or absolutely, nothing

  - o **Yet all of them would have a massively beneficial effect on every child in the classroom**

But it IS also about funding ..

- Successive UK Governments (certainly up until the 2024 election) actively chose to spend far too little on every single area of education, for far too long

  - o They particularly spent too little on Special Educational Needs and Disabilities, on specialist support, on in-school training, on specialist settings, on support staff, on facilities, on social care, on health care ..

    you name it, if it's got anything to do with SEND, it's screaming out for more practitioners, more settings, and more funding

- So-called "Safety Valve" or "Delivering Better Value" agreements are NOT the answer!

  o Need is not about "value" or "budget" or keeping Councils "safe"
  o Need is need
  o Need costs
  o And need **must** be provided for under the law

Council officers, education staff, teachers, school governors, even TAs are ALL Public Servants
- Public Servants work for the public – NOT the other way round
- Public Servants are obliged to always strive to uphold **The Nolan Principles of Public Life:**
  o Selflessness
  o Integrity
  o Objectivity
  o Accountability
  o Honesty
  o Openness
  o Leadership

  But over my 11 years as a SEND parent, I have met far too many TAs, Teachers, SENCOs, Head Teachers, Governors and Local Authority Officers **who have NO CONCEPT of their duty of "public service"** whatsoever.

If councils are going bankrupt because they do not have enough money to provide lawfully-required services, THAT IS NOT the end service-needers fault
- It is a failure of lawful duty, on the part of Local Authorities to

  o Understand and accept their lawful commitments to SEND children o Hold successive central Governments to account, where those Governments failed to provide enough money for lawfully-required services and provision

- A council going bankrupt is a failure of policy, and of governance, at <u>every</u> level. **It is NOT, I repeat <u>NOT</u>, the fault of SEND families**

Stop blaming SEND children for breaking
- Bad policy is not children's fault
- Bad governance is not children's fault
- Failure to make lawfully-required provision is not children's fault
- Teachers failing to be properly trained in SEND, and so not recognising the needs in their classroom, is not children's fault
- The mental health crisis amongst school-age children is not children's fault
- Harm being caused to children's mental wellbeing, just because they are children with Special Educational Needs and/or Disabilities, is not their fault
- Expressing the harm they are experiencing by collapsing with extreme anxiety, falling into school distress, and being unable to attend school anymore because of that harm, <u>is not children's fault</u>

Stop blaming SEND parents
- Bad policy, lack of teacher training, lack of funding for SEND, the national collapse of CAMHS services, and the harm being caused to our children **is not our fault, any more than it is our children's**

- Our children have had SEND from the day they born and they will have these same needs until the end of their days: parents have not "concocted" our children's needs just for "fun"

- **We remove our children from school for their protection, and because there is no other choice left**
    - Any other loving and engaged parent would do exactly the same – i.e. protect their child - if they were faced with our position

More than that, STOP BLAMING SEND MUMS

- It is most often mums who are fighting for their SEND children's rights under the law. Many of us are fighting alone and unsupported

- **The open misogyny we face in this system every day is as blatant as it is appalling**

- The misogyny comes from male as well as female staff, both in schools and in LAs; the unspoken insinuation is that SEND mums are "making stuff up" about our kids, that we are "too sensitive", "over-invested" or are essentially "hysterical"

    - As a perfect example, one parent told me about a SEND meeting they attended in school where the head looked from the mum to the dad, and told the dad "I've always found you, dad, to be very reasonable .."

- As another example, in 2024 Warwickshire Councillors Jeff Morgan and Claire Golby were on record suggesting rising demand might not necessarily mean there was "genuine need", and suggested council leaders needed to start asking 'tougher', 'more penetrating' questions.

    - Cllr Clare Golby, said: "I think one of the questions is what comes down to parenting and what comes down to 'SEND issues'.

- o Cllr Morgan said the Council should be: "... not automatically accepting **the pleas of a mother** saying that 'little Willy' has got ADHD, when in actual fact, little Willy is just really badly behaved and needs some form of strict correction."

- I rest my case on this one: the judgement and misogyny we face is utterly insidious, vicious, underhand, overwhelming. **It has to stop**

Stop criminalising SEND parents
- Protecting our children from harm is <u>not</u> a criminal offence
- It has to stop being treated as if it is, with
    - Fines
    - Court appearances
    - Threats of prison
    - Police turning up or Social Services removing children from families – families who did nothing but try to protect their child from the harm they had experienced in school

When parents made a choice to send our children to school, we did <u>not</u> make a choice for our children to be harmed there
- That such harm happens at all, in any school anywhere, is where the <u>real</u> "crime" lies

Just like our children, SEND parents are coming to a great deal of harm
- Many parents of SEND children have unknown or undiagnosed SEND of our own

- Whether we have SEND or not, when The System fails our children, parents' mental health and wellbeing are just as impacted as our children's
  - The gaslighting, open hostility and Systems Generated Trauma we face from schools, governors, and from Local Authorities, is utterly overwhelming and utterly devastating

  - But that damage to parental mental health has gone **completely unacknowledged** for decades

  - The University of Birmingham published their study into the suicide risk in parent carers in July 2024.

  - To reiterate that study, it found "41% of parents in England who have a child with a long-term illness or disability have thought about suicide whilst caring for their child" (Source: http://www.birmingham.ac.uk/news/2024/more-than-40-of-parents-with-disabled-children-have-thought-about-suicide-study)

  - Until the July 2024 election, the only answers the UK government came up with, were to:
    - double down on academisation, the national curriculum and SATS
    - apportion yet more blame to parents
    - further demonise Elective Home Education
    - enforce more fines and prosecutions
    - attempt an ill-advised, ill-fated and ultimately pointless SEND Review in 2023
    - bring in so-called "Safety Valve" / "Delivering Better Value" agreements – agreements which were specifically designed to cut spending and SEND children's access to the EHCPs, provision and services they are lawfully entitled to, even further

- crack down even harder on enforced attendance (without understanding what the issues behind non-attendance really were)

- And at the time of writing this book, new Education Secretary Bridget Philipson was <u>still</u> insisting that 100% attendance is the answer, and that school is "the best place" for every child

Enforced Attendance is not an answer!

- 100% attendance, which schools and policy makers remain so fixated on, is <u>not</u> an indicator of future academic success or failure:
  - It is an indicator who is the most compliant, who never gets ill, or who is best at masking. Nothing more

- Enforced attendance masks the real problem anyway!
  - Just because a child is physically in school, does not mean they feel safe and able – or are being genuinely supported – to learn

    - Many SEND children spend their days in isolation pods, because they cannot cope in the classroom, **and schools have nowhere else to put them**

    - Most children in those situations are receiving no teaching input, no support, nothing. They are literally just ticking a register box, and taking up space.

    - The child is in school, they are "attending" .. but they are learning nothing, and receiving no specialist intervention whatsoever. I've even been told via my blog about high school-age kids being given colouring in to do, just to fill the time. No. Words.

- Additionally, "We cannot deliver provision if you are not sending your child to school.." is coercive, family-blaming crap. Stop it!
  - If schools were delivering the right provision, children would not be collapsing out of school in crisis

"Fit in or F-off" is not an answer either

- Children of all ages desperately want and deserve to feel happy, safe and welcome in the place where they do their learning

- The majority of SEND children desperately want

  - to be in a school or learning environment they can call their own, where they feel they are wanted, where they can make friends, and where they feel they belong
  - to access an education that meets their needs

- SEND parents want the same

  - Most SEND kids could be OK in mainstream schools, IF those schools adapted teaching to what actual children's needs really are – both with and without SEND
  - But right now, SEND parents and our children cannot fit in; The System and the policies within that system, are deliberately designed that way

Stop framing NEED as "demand" - #1

- SEND families are not deliberately breaking a "social contract" when it comes to education

- The schools that do the harm, and the policy makers who created the current system, are breaking the "social contract" of education with us

Stop framing NEED as "demand" - #2

- Parents are not "being pushy", "asking too much", making "unreasonable demands", or creating noise for the sake of it

- We are only asking for our children to be mentally and emotionally safe in school, and for The Law to be upheld

Stop framing NEED as "demand" - #3

- The UK does not have anywhere near enough specialist SEND settings. Plain and simple.

- The LA-run special schools we do have are insufficiently funded, oversubscribed, overloaded, and are also often nowhere near specific enough:

  o For example, a SEND child with a profound, inward and/or mute presentation of their needs is never going to survive emotionally (or any better than in a mainstream school), if they are placed in the same setting as children with profoundly outward presentations of need that include shouting, aggression, self harming or unintentional violence against others

  o It is not making a "demand" to state that fact: it's telling the truth about NEED

Stop framing NEED as "demand" - #4

- NEED is fluid; levels of it, and the types of presentation, can change from year to year
- That means the service response may need to change from year to year
- And that means budgets are inevitably going to fall/rise in response
- Policy makers hate that need cannot be quantified in a spreadsheet or controlled with a budget
- Policy makers also hate the fact that Special Educational Needs and/or Disabilities **automatically cost more money to support** than "one size fits all"

  - "One size fits all" is a lie: it does not fit all!

  - Whether policy makers or budget controllers can quantify it or not, and whether they like or not, meeting needs takes political will, **and it costs money**

  - Policy makers and budget controllers must accept that reality! It is NOT a choice.

Need must be met under the Law! And the underpinning SEND Laws have not changed

  - At the time of writing this book, no Parliament has altered the Equality Act 2010 or the Children and Families Act 2014, or any of the other key legislation that makes up the inter-connected web that is SEND law. They are all still in force and have not been changed:
  - Not by any budgetary decisions
  - Not by policies like "austerity" or "streamlining"
  - Not by any "Safety Valve" agreement designed to cut costs
  - Not even during the Covid pandemic

No-one is above the Law. Yet pretty much EVERYONE with the power in The System <u>acts as if they are</u>

- SEND parents find time and time again that no matter how hard we try to have the law enforced on our children's behalf, we cannot. Because no-one in power is accepting responsibility:

  - not teachers
  - not SENCOs
  - not Heads
  - not Governors
  - not Commissioning Teams in Councils
  - not councillors, council leaders, Service Directors or Chief Executives
  - not even the DfE

- During the previous Government, even the DfE was failing to accept its lawful responsibility, and was trying to enforce "Safety Valve" agreements right up to its last days in power

- Yet in July 2024, as Garden Court Chambers reported on their blog, the High Court "... **reaffirms that local authorities are under 'absolute duty' to secure special educational provision and grants a mandatory order**"

- (Source: https://www.gardencourtchambers.co.uk/news/high-court-reaffirms-that-local-authorities-are-under-absolute-duty-to-secure-special-educational-provision-and-grants-a-mandatory-order#:~:text=Immigration%20Blog-,High%20Court%20reaffirms%20that%20local%20authorities%20are%20under%20'absolute%20duty,and%20grants%20a%20mandatory%20order)

High Court reaffirms that local authorities are under 'absolute duty' to secure special educational provision and grants a mandatory order

MONDAY 29 JULY 2024

- **SEND law, and SEND provision, are <u>NOT optional</u>!**
  - Policy makers, educators, LAs and everyone involved in the SEND circle <u>must</u> accept their lawful obligations

"Safety Valve" Agreements MUST be scrapped

- Government telling councils to cut costs by cutting access to SEND services that families are lawfully entitled to, IS UNLAWFUL

- Stop these "agreements" and reverse them right now:
  - no-one, from Gillian Keegan as Secretary of State for Education, to Council Chief Execs and Service Directors had the right to introduce them, or to try to impose their devastating effects on SEND families
  - And no-one has the lawful right to now keep them in place

Because, once more for clarity: SEND LAW <u>has not changed</u>!

- The <u>only</u> thing that has changed over consecutive governments, is <u>policy</u> – and policy is NOT the same as LAW

- After the Gove reforms in 2014, there was <u>no</u> cohesive approach to Education Policy whatsoever:

  - Between 2010 and 2024, the UK had a revolving door of 10 Education Secretaries in 13 years
    (Source: https://news.sky.com/story/the-revolving-door-of-education-secretaries-has-created-an-environment-as-stable-as-crumbling-concrete-12957416)

  - Is there any wonder we had what Bridget Philipson, the then-Shadow Education

Secretary, speaking at the Centre for Social Justice in Jan 2024, described as:

"A curriculum that narrows, not broadens our children's experiences and opportunities, where the pursuit of high standards has become too often synonymous with joylessness, when nothing of the sort need be true."
(Source:https://schoolsweek.co.uk/phillipson-invokes-zeal-of-gove-reforms-in-labour-schools-vision/)

The "SEND Emergency" is the symptom. The actual sickness is in The System

- From years of misguided, dogmatic education policy..
- To the way Local Authorities handle SEND ...
- To how School Governors fail/are unable to hold schools to account ...
- Right the way down to how teachers are cultivated by their training, their utter lack of SEND knowledge, their professional indifference, arrogance and "group think" ..
- Plus the rigours and demands that Quality First Teaching places on children, and the "combat stress" effects of Command and Control ...
- **All of this must be accepted as where the real problem lies**

"Intelligence Cleansing" of SEND children has to stop. Full stop.

- Mainstream schools - both Academies and Local Authority-controlled settings - **are actively forcing SEND families out**

- This practice is not just morally wrong: it is 100% unlawful
    - o Schools and Local Authorities both know that

o Yet both are causing "Intelligence Cleansing" to happen - when they know there is nowhere else for SEND children to go

o **In far too many cases, "elective home education" has not been an "elective" choice at all:** families have been forced to go down that route, whether it was the right one or not – because school became so intolerable, so punishing and crushing, there was no other option left

Local Authorities are completely the wrong body to oversee EHCPs

- Most EHCPs are nothing more than an admin exercise:
  - o Many EHCPs are written by untrained staff with no knowledge of real SEND need, **or the law that applies to it**

  - o Many EHCPs are written deliberately vaguely, without SMART (Specific, Measurable, Achievable, Realistic & Time-bound) outcomes

  - o **Even before the "Safety Valve" agreements began, most EHCPs were written to suit the LAs budget**, rather than what children's needs really were

    - ▪ Many EHCPs have nothing more than the most basic funding attached – no matter how great the child's need actually is

  - o All of the above make the Plan completely unenforceable / not worth the paper it is written on. This practice is unlawful.

- LAs rely on
  - parents trusting them to be the experts they ought to be
  - parents not knowing what a robust, well written Plan should look like, or what it should contain

- They also rely on parents being so grateful to finally have a Plan that they will not argue about what's actually in it

- And they rely on parents being too scared of The System, to lodge an appeal with the Tribunal and get a failing Plan re-written

- **The First Tier Tribunal upholds over 95%* of appeals in favour of SEND families, and against LAs** .. yet LAs keep on trying the same tricks/applying the same level of indifference and unlawfulness to EHCPs, in the hope of getting away with it

  (* - See this excellent article from Special Needs Jungle to find out more about Tribunals: https://www.specialneedsjungle.com/send-tribunal-2023-councils-stop-wasting-public-funds-send-appeals-fail-almost-all-time/)

SEND families need an independent "police force"
- If you or I do something unlawful, there is an automatic consequence

- Yet schools and LAs act unlawfully towards SEND families <u>every day of the year</u>
  - They do so knowingly, and in the full confidence that no-one is ever really going to hold them to account - because the majority of families have no means of seeking a redress for what has unlawfully happened to their SEND children

- ○ When families do try to take a legal route – either via First Tier Tribunal, or Judicial Review, Schools double down even harder on "intelligence cleansing" practices, to make the problem go away. Even just trying to talk about our experiences is met with a disproportionate level of hostility:
    - ▪ I've heard via my blog of parents being told by schools "all bets are off" (or words to that effect) if they sought legal advice, **or if they even spoke to other parents**

- ○ LAs will deliberately and cynically stretch out or distort the process
    - • to save money on another year of funding
    - • to make sure the child "ages out" and is no longer entitled to the support being sought

    OR

    - • To make sure the family runs out of money to fight and/or cannot access Legal Aid on behalf of their child

- • Families need an independent body to whom we can turn: one with statutory powers to oversee, quality assure and enforce lawful SEND provision, both in schools and within LAs

Policymakers: Stop trying to solve a problem you don't actually understand

- • If policy comes from the wrong place, or with the wrong intention, it is never going to work

- • If policy is unlawful, it can never work

- • Yet time after time, policy makers, ministers and educators have tried to force solutions on education

and/or "the SEND crisis", without ever truly understanding
- o how the crisis in schools, education and SEND happened in the first place

  OR

- o that what they are trying to enforce is actually unlawful

"We are not seeing it" is <u>not</u> an answer!

- If policy makers, educators and LAs "Are Not Seeing" the problem in mainstream education
  - o they are not looking through the right lens
  - o or they are not asking the right questions
  - o **or they are deliberately ignoring the problem**

- The evidence that the current system is not working is all around, it is in plain sight, and that evidence is growing by the day as more and more children collapse out of that system

The answers SEND families need are NOT going to come from The System

- The System has proven that it cannot and will not regulate itself

- The changes The System needs will – just like the removal of corporal punishment from schools – be ultimately be driven by <u>parents</u> ... **whether The System likes that or not!**

- SEND families have knowledge and genuine, lived experience that will help policy makers and educators understand what ours and our children's realities are

- SEND families currently exist in a policy vacuum: most of it was <u>never</u> created with SEND families in mind

- We can help to change that! Thousands of us have tried to engage with policy makers via petitions, attendance at Parliamentary committees, working with journalists, writing books, talking to councillors, contacting our MPs, blogging, creating podcasts, even marching on the street

  o Yet we, and our children, and their needs, have been consistently ignored

- You need our knowledge about what our children really need, to know where to direct resources, and how to frame the solutions

- **But more importantly, you need our buy-in**

  o Our trust has been utterly destroyed, because we and our children are being utterly destroyed

SEND parents will <u>not</u> stop fighting until this abusive and abhorrent situation changes for our children
- We were <u>forced</u> to begin fighting The System
- We were <u>forced</u> to become far more knowledgeable about SEND, and SEND law, than most of the so-called "experts" who make decisions about us and our families

- **We cannot now afford to stop that fight**

  o for ourselves and for our children

  o and for parents and children who haven't even entered The System yet, but who are also going to be harmed by that System <u>if it does not change</u>

Childhood is short. Children are too precious, their minds are too precious, and their futures are too precious to allow this systematic harm to keep happening to yet another generation.

But until SEND families can once again trust in the mainstream education system, and trust that <u>all</u> children will be safe there, this problem is not going away.

And neither are we.

LUISA GRAY

WE ARE NOT SEEING IT

About the Author

Luisa Gray (a.k.a LongRoadSENDMum) is proud parent to two fantastic kids, who also happen to have SEND (Special Educational Needs & Disabilities).

After careering around a bit in advertising, and nearly losing her mind as a stay-at-home mum, Luisa became a parent blogger. Parenting hadn't turned out to quite like it looked in the glossy baby magazines (because let's be honest, none of those glossy magazines ever talk about "What to do if it turns out your kiddo has SEND and you worked that out but nobody believes you").

Sharing her experiences of this unexpected SEND journey with - and giving support to - other families in the same situation, was basically cheaper than therapy. It's also brought a lot of joy and connection with thousands of other parents in the same situation.

"The Long Road – A Diary of a SEND Mum" has been running on Facebook since 2021, organically growing a loyal following of nearly 10,000 SEND parents, practitioners and professionals from all over the world. People are drawn to Luisa's informal, warm, sometimes funny, sometimes angry, but always no-gloss and truthful approach to life as a UK SEND parent. For some reason, people also seem to really like her hand-drawn "crap sketches".

Luisa lives in the North of England with LongRoadDad, Big Bruv, Little Sis and probably one too many cats. She likes loud music, strong tea and good cake.

Printed in Great Britain
by Amazon